From prehistoric cave art to abstract expressionism, from the Orient to the Western world —the six volumes in this series provide a panoramic view of man's achievements and his aspirations as they have been expressed in painting. The illustrations, all in full color, have been chosen with an eye to their freshness as well as their intrinsic worth: many of these masterpieces are virtually inaccessible to even the most dedicated art lover. Each volume is introduced by a leading authority in the field, who presents his insights in lucid, simple prose. Hans L. C. Jaffé, Professor of Modern Art at the University of Amsterdam, has edited the series with knowledge and care, to make *20,000 Years of World Painting* both a major esthetic experience and an exciting introduction to the history of art. The volumes in the series are:

P. FRANCASTEL

Medieval Painting

EDITED BY *Hans L. C. Jaffé*
TRANSLATED BY *Robert Erich Wolf*

20,000 Years of World Painting

VOLUME II

LAUREL EDITION

Published by
DELL PUBLISHING CO., INC.
750 Third Avenue
New York, New York 10017

Laurel ® TM 674623, Dell Publishing Co., Inc.

Originally published as part of one volume
entitled 20,000 YEARS OF WORLD PAINTING

Reprinted by arrangement with
Harry N. Abrams, Incorporated

Manufactured in the Netherlands

First printing—1968

INTRODUCTION

The whole notion of the "Middle Ages" bids fair to go out of fashion. It belongs to ways of thinking of other ages than ours. Men felt in the Renaissance that, after dark centuries of ignorance, they were reforging the link with the only form of civilization which had permitted man to express the eternal values inherent in human nature: the classical past. In the nineteenth century, when Western man was beginning to think of himself as the standard-bearer of evolution and progress rather than as a mere detail in a history of dates and facts, the historian Michelet still insisted that there were three contrasting phases: the first developing according to the natural order of history; the second, a grandiose adventure of the spirit led on by the mirage of the invisible; and the third—come to triumph after the French Revolution—presaging for a second time a new development in the natural order of life.

The West has not only conquered the planet by force of arms, it has also convinced all mankind of the superiority of its intellectual techniques as the one way to grasp and hold control of the terrestrial stage where man acts out his gallant epic. But this means also that the West can never again view itself in quite the same perspectives as of old. In the first place, the very act of imposing on other peoples its own modes of technical organization as the sole guide to prosperity has led the West to discover that in the realm of knowledge there exist other values, other modalities than its own. Simultaneously, it has deepened the understanding to be gained by its native methods of reflection and analysis and has also transformed its own grasp of problems on the levels of both physical causality and conceptual relationships. Embracing an incredibly multiplied number of phenomena both in time and space, extending its knowledge to both the infinitely great and the infinitely minute, the West has armed itself during the past half century with new tools of thought as well as new techniques of action.

The result: our past appears to us in new perspectives. It is no longer possible for us to carry on with the idea that the development of human consciousness has taken place in a straight line only, and that that line has been the only valid form of thought 5 throughout all time and for all men and all societies. One of the casualties has been the notion of the "Middle Ages," at least in the sense the term has had for the past five centuries and in spite of whatever bits and pieces of lasting truth it may still express.

The text you have in hand has no ambition to rewrite the history of a whole millennium. Much more modest, it wishes only to tell about artworks produced in the West between the birth of the Christian world and the Italian Renaissance, and it still thinks of that "rebirth" as a time which initiated a new mastery of thought and generated a universalism comparable only to that of the ancient classical world and, even more, to that of Neolithic times when a single culture budded everywhere on our planet.

Certainly these few pages cannot provide a complete gallery of all the significant artworks of those twelve or fourteen centuries of development and change. The mere act of selecting them would demand long and patient study based on a new and special view of history. What is more, by their very nature there are limitations on the works that can be reproduced. Stained glass can really be shown only schematically, with no more than its lines and composition brought out clearly. No reproduction, however fine, can ever bring out the fact that, in a church enshrined by a shell of colored glass, the function of the windows is not to offer to the eyes merely another set of scenes to decipher, similar to and interchangeable with those displayed in cycles of frescoes or miniatures; rather, those windows are there to bring to life the interior space of the church with its hourly metamorphoses in light and expressiveness. It is unfortunate, but true, that a reproduction necessarily detaches one element from the ensemble for which it was conceived and thereby alters the appearance and meaning of any artwork. An album of images such as this cannot pretend to put into your grasp ensembles as they truly are or were, but only to furnish a key to let you into their few corners which are most easily accessible to our present state of understanding.

In our times, the image is *à la mode*. There is no dearth of books which make an ever larger place for the image as a clue to how things were in past ages. There are writers who fancy they have revealed something about art when they include in their books a great number of fragmentary reproductions of details as corroboration of events and principles already amply documented in their written sources. True, one can never avoid isolating the parts from the whole—by definition impossible to represent—when one tries to bring out those elements one judges significant for one's own attempt to interpret the values of the past. But it 6 must always be kept in mind that the books we create cannot really reconstruct ensembles now dispersed and forever lost to us in their original state, and this despite the fact that the eye gives us the means to grasp aspects of reality, past or present, inaccessible to all other procedures of observation and study. And yet, if we toy with the notion that any and every fragment of figurative art belongs to a universal museum in which it may be switched about as fancy wills from one civilization to another, with no thought for the role it played or plays within a determined system, and if we blithely ignore the simple fact that to understand any work of art involves understanding the logic indigenous to the milieu which made it and to which it once belonged, we merely accumulate documents without gaining any insight either into the original value of such works or into what they can reveal of the mechanisms of thought characteristic of a limited and well-defined period in history. In the final analysis then, one derives from those artworks no more than the substratum our age holds in common with all other ages; history is shrunken to an exercise in artificial and sterile erudition in which the very notion is lost of reconstructing the wholes belonging to other times or places, together with any possibility of understanding how men's thoughts have guided their hands.

Our aim in this book is not so pretentious. Allowing for the inevitable limitations on procuring photographs of every work we should have liked to include, we have kept our choice to paintings, in the broader sense of the word: that is, to mosaics, frescoes, miniatures, and the portable pictures on wood which were the ancestors of modern easel paintings. On the other hand, we have not been content with merely a garland of what today are taken to be the "world's great paintings." Instead, we have selected in such a way as to disclose the guiding thread for those who wish to go farther and deeper. On the basis of what has been said above, I hope to show that in the course of the period between the end of the ancient world and the full upsurge (rather than the bare beginnings) of the Italian Renaissance the function of painting changed at least twice. I do not personally consider figurative art as the external manifestation of a universal faculty all men possess and utilize in the same fashion and for the same purposes in all societies, past and present. Thus it seemed to me that this book offered a happy occasion to show in a modest way, but with precision, the value of painting as an instrument of culture, as a visual expression of thought.

In its earliest phase, medieval painting and Christian painting were one and the same. Certainly the Christians did not all at once work out an original new system of figurative representation. 7

As always happens, to express new values they employed the old means society already had at hand. The first Christians were converted pagans; their painting likewise was a pagan painting diverted from its contemporaneous significance. This meant that the artists' first task was to work out a new iconography. Where they were able to speak their faith boldly and aloud—in the catacombs—they established new symbolic signs for their new creed. The usual inscriptions on tombs soon came to be accompanied by visual symbols: first, conventional figures posed as if in prayer; then more specific attributes; finally—very soon as a matter of fact—genuine pictorial images such as the Good Shepherd and the Virgin and Child came to embody the key moments of the legend which was gradually taking shape. From the outset Christian painting expressed above all the fundamental belief in another existence in which the individual believer does not lose his identity. In the catacombs such painting was buried from the public eye as Egyptian painting once had been, but unlike Egyptian painting it represented a common destiny and as a result was highly generalized in character. Only very much later did it depict particular saints, the witnesses to a faith which, at the start, was spread as a direct message from the original proselytes. It was a painting of faith and hope, the tangible expression of a spiritual attitude. Later it was employed to make the rites more vivid, as well as, in addition to the rites themselves, the events and acts by which faith manifested itself more and more: first the sacred writings were illustrated, then the heroic deeds of the faithful were commemorated. After having begun as an expression of man's inward hope, Christian painting went on to bear witness, to enshrine tradition and history. It became, then, a new intellectual system modifying both the individual representation of destiny as well as the causality of the acts men perform. In short, it helped give stability first to a state of mind, a spiritual tradition, and then to the entire tradition of the faithful. In this way it created both a durable record of human feeling and a history quite apart from official history. It offered to artists—and through them to the faithful—a painstakingly worked-out repertory of attitudes and events which could have meaning only for the initiated. It is not surprising, therefore, that at the outset Christian painting consisted of only the scantiest subject matter. But in time it became the immense common depository of the concepts and memories of individuals who were otherwise strangers to each other in all their ways of doing and of thinking. As a consequence, Christian painting presents not a documentation of the manners, modes of life, and outward 8 actions of the society which brought it into being, but the working-out of a system of communicable signs and symbols whose secret cannot be grasped by the uninitiated.

Not that Christian art rejected the means of pagan painting to achieve this end. The Christian painters of the first epoch were Roman in dress and manners, and lived in dwellings decorated in Hellenistic styles, and they kept up the techniques and figurative elements the dominant civilization equipped them with. Since their first task was not to furnish the powers-that-be with new art forms designed to persuade the masses to specific thoughts or acts, at the outset the painters did not even try to depict any society other than the civil society of their time. Later, when Christianity became the official creed of the Roman Empire, it was only natural that art should aspire to express the imperial will, which was to guarantee the conversion of all contemporary society with the minimum possible disturbance to things as they were. That is why, in Rome as in Salonica, the first great ensembles exposed to public gaze show us the Romans changed in their hearts, as it were, but not in their outward aspects. In the mosaics of San Lorenzo in Milan the Ancestors of Christ are draped in togas, as is Moses in the mosaics of Santa Maria Maggiore in Rome. It took centuries for a very small number of symbols to become immediately comprehensible to the public. For in no epoch does a figurative art develop merely through the rapid proliferation of its signs and motifs. Styles are based on a deepening of the possibilities opened up by a system, not on the dissemination throughout a culture of certain signs arrived at by an intellectual principle whereby everyone can translate at sight and automatically those signs into elements filled with meaning. For this reason, Christian art was concerned neither with illusionism nor with startling innovations. On the contrary, it became a conventional code in which, over and over again, a very few essential themes and figurative formulas were more and more deeply explored.

From its beginnings, however, Christian painting hesitated between two paths. Alien as it was to any kind of illusionism and to realism, it began by giving material form to certain intellectual concepts, by visualizing them, as it were. From that point it went on to recount the events which were part of a history at that time still "modern." For a millennium the Christian legend was to play the role played by Homer's poetry or the Vedas in other civilizations or, to a lesser degree but in like manner, by the French romances of the Round Table. As it happened, those epics were transmitted through literary and not pictorial channels, and the question arises as to how much the extraordinary hold Christianity came to exercise may have been due to the fact that, 9 by preference, it utilized visual images to implant its message in the minds of men.

At the outset, Christian painting—a secret, indeed a stealthy art—made use of the frescoed wall painting as its means of expression. In its earliest phase it did not seek to profit from the abundant resources of contemporary art, restricting itself in the catacombs to fixing a small number of simple, isolated images with no concern for the decoration of the total environment. As a second step it had recourse to the art of mosaic. Once the Church had made its peace with the Roman Empire, Christian art became the official art and benefited from the wealth that power brought. At the same time, its content changed. Instead of recording the intimate hopes of the faithful, it proclaimed aloud the doctrine of power. The hidden art became a public art and expressed the will of great princes to establish among their peoples a single unified belief. Very soon, as in Ravenna, it held up before the Christian flock the register of all those virtues considered indispensable to social cohesion. Rather than insisting on the purely religious bond which unites each of us to the Unknown, it gave concrete form to the positive truths on which rests the solidarity of the members of a well-disciplined social body. In the mosaics of Ravenna the Emperor was held up as a necessary factor in the right sort of belief, during a long period in which divergent orthodoxies clashed head on. As generations slipped by, art became more of an instrument of intellectual understanding than a soul-stirring witness to the timorous but often heroic faith of individuals that it once had been.

It is no more than fair to insist on the high quality of Christian mosaics of the earliest Middle Ages. In Rome, Salonica, and Ravenna, a technique was worked out during four centuries which was far superior to that of any known works during antiquity. The artists employed color with consummate mastery and created ensembles whose beauty is quite independent of their intellectual message. Indeed, the beauty of those great ensembles is entirely unlike the immobile and serene perfection of classical Greek art, but it is as high a summit of the emotional power of fascination that the representation in color of an imaginary universe always carries with it. The splendor of Christian mosaics surpasses by far what the technique of antiquity could achieve and bears witness to the high spirituality of the age. Today, through our familiarity with this art, we have at last come to understand that the innumerable quarrels of the theologians—so "Byzantine" to the modern mind—were the expression of brave controversies in which individuals not only staked 10 everything on the acceptance or rejection of some doctrinal definition, but also brought into play their spiritual being. Theology in that age was man's central concern, as humanism and mathematics were later to become and, in our time, physics and its various ways of depicting the universe. With no more than tiny cubes of marble subtly cut and matched, artists succeeded in preserving for us some reflection of the glory of Justinian and Theodora; at the same time, they made tangible to us a system which, for all its hierarchies, set up a perfectly organic conception of the universe. It would be ingratitude on our part to fail to recognize that in those few images, easy to comprehend as well as deeply expressive, they bequeathed to us documents of their age unmatched by anything we can read in the chronicles and texts of the time. A rigid religion based on the terror of men in awe before the ministers of a God who was not satisfied with promising them fair judgment at the end, but lay upon them the burden of submitting meekly here on earth to all His rites and rituals— what a vast change from the simple faith of the catacombs! Implicit already in the first centuries of our era is the second phase of Christian art.

Between the fourth and eighth centuries, painting was at first militant, then triumphant; first the expression of the hopes for the miraculous of a minority of believers, later the finest tool of government in the hands of a theocracy that sought to impose at least some fugitive unity on its subjects. This unity was made the more necessary on the spiritual level by the fragility of the political ties which bound men to each other. Although as early as the fifth century invasions had broken the frontiers' of the Empire, the Roman world continued to absorb new peoples, thanks chiefly to that religion rooted in the common people and tinged with the miraculous which Rome had seen fit to adopt when the time was ripe. The last bastions were not shattered until the eighth century, and then only by a new wave of invasions brought on by the awakening of the Arab world, and by the pressure of Central Asia on the Middle East. Only then did the unity of the Mediterranean world fall asunder and the ties which held society together go slack. The general splintering of the world led also to the splintering and definitive collapse of the framework of Christian culture inasmuch as it had made of its institutions one basic element of human order. Material ruin decimated the workshops of the refined art of mosaic, intellectual ruin destroyed the last vestiges of unity in the ancient world. Then, for more than five centuries, there were no more great undertakings comparable to those which were the glory of Salonica and Ravenna. And yet, curious as it seems, the great art of mosaic was not destined to disappear. After a few centuries it would once again produce splendid works, as soon as a semblance of organization was set up after the expulsion of the invading hordes. In the twelfth century in Venice, as in Sicily and Constantinople and later, in the fourteenth century, in Greece, new and admirable monumental ensembles were created that were the direct continuation of the great Byzantine works of the century of Justinian. No human tradition is ever wholly lost in the sands of time when cataclysms strike, nothing disappears merely because it is worn out. Humanity forgets nothing. Values suffer eternal eclipse only when replaced by other values. Man does not humbly efface himself save when other men impose a new and alien order on the places he has settled and cherished. One of the great errors of the science of history is to seek chronological dividing-posts between civilizations. At no time does a society live entirely in the past or in the future, and the present is never anything but a fragile equilibrium between the two. Thus, though Christian imagery had been evolved in the historic period when the state religion, Christianity, was incarnated in works proclaiming the triumph of dogma, for many centuries it was still able to engender new masterpieces wherever a civil organization more or less faithfully modeled after the former type came into being.

And yet it is also true that a new form of culture and of Christian art began to take shape, beginning in the eighth and ninth centuries. This form was destined to have a no less lengthy and brilliant future. In the West, Christian art of this second phase belonged to a clerical civilization, and it manifested itself first in manuscript illuminations, then in frescoes.

Just as no civilization can vanish suddenly, neither can it emerge unprepared. It simply does not happen that on some particular day and by some stroke of genius a society can invent the form and content of a new culture. Evolution is continuous; man never tosses away *en masse* all the cultural apparatus on hand. Every object, every form, every symbol constitutes a point of encounter and interpenetration of many levels of consciousness combined in diverse modes of significance and with variable aims. When one has shown that a particular graphic device or practice had already been conceived within a particular system, one cannot conclude that one has thereby disclosed the source of new ideas, the prototype which inspired a new culture. The elements are not what counts, but only how they are put together. Some practice, device, or object which within a particular context played no more than a secondary role suddenly becomes the basic principle

12 of a new organization incarnating new and original values full of

promise for the future. In this way, the clerical civilization which arose in the West early in the eighth century borrowed most of its tools from the past, but to each of these tools it imparted a new significance because it had itself instituted a new human order on both the intellectual and social planes.

It was certainly not Carolingian civilization that invented manuscripts. But it is beyond question that it was that civilization which made them the chief instrument for the dissemination of learning. The true revolution in the Occident dates from the time when in the monasteries—the only centers of organization and the only repositories of learning during the dark centuries of the breakup of the Empire and invasions from abroad—it was discovered that everything known could be preserved and transmitted in texts and images. It was then (and, in particular, in the entourage of Charlemagne) that Western civilization—modern civilization—found the way to its astonishing future. At that time the West was neither more advantageously situated nor more advanced than other civilizations. But it did understand the power that derives from pinning down facts and from the effective presentation of the truth, or of what passes for truth. With the organization of the scriptoria—workshops of scribes— and the imposition of the Carolingian script, Charlemagne gave to the West the first two weapons for its conquest of intellectual leadership. We still write in the script he championed, and it is but a short time since we have ceased to look at the world as he did. Gutenberg and the development of engraving, six centuries later, mark the moment when those two chief instruments of the concrete culture of the spirit became widely diffused and our modern world began. But credit for the actual invention, the innovation, belongs to the Carolingian world, and not by accident. Quite the contrary. It was the result of the coming together of the finest minds of a time, and it had the merit of discovering some of those simple things to which men, after a few centuries of familiarity, have become so accustomed that they no longer even notice them. So true is this that today certain younger historians catering to the popular taste can dare to assert in flashy vacuous writings that history could well do without Charlemagne, that too much, to their way of thinking, has been made of him.

The need to restore culture to a ravaged world even while it was still strife-torn made the value of books much more evident, and this was recognized as early as the seventh century. This was a period of missionary zeal, set upon rescuing the essential values from oblivion. The Irish monks already looked on books as one and the same thing as the Word of the Gospels. For them a book 13 was a treasure, something with an existence of its own, living and personal. As early as this was launched the process of identification of thought with its vehicle, the sign. Linked with the Roman tradition, the Irish monks took one of the very first steps toward the Carolingian renaissance. A second step was taken a little later, in Northumbria, toward a closer bond between the graphic character of the image and script itself. But it was at the court of Charlemagne that men foregathered from England, Ireland, Italy, Spain, and France, from the banks of the Loire as from those of the Rhine. It was these men who gave the impulse not to a mere revival of antique culture but, rather, to the possibility of something new, a different and unique culture. From that standpoint, it is clear that, although the term "renaissance" applies less accurately to the Carolingian revival than to the later Humanist movement, this in no way detracts—indeed, quite the contrary—from the great creative achievement of the epoch. Within the Carolingian perspective, which was that of a Christian Empire, there could be no question of a return to the culture of pagan antiquity: men dreamed of Constantine, not Augustus, and they sought to fasten on what was permanent, not to cancel out a cycle of history. For the Carolingians there could be only a single Truth. The conflicts which were to arise between the ecclesiastical and military powers were not a question of the proper sharing of authority but, instead, of which single authority should triumph in the end.

Just as in the first phase, painting in the new period was to play a role so much the greater because the number of sources of learning were few. With no more than the Scriptures to go on, iconography could not depend on a diversity of themes but only on the high quality of the work achieved. In complete opposition to the ideal of monumental painting, the Carolingian clerks created in their manuscript illuminations an art which, although in a different context, is as perfect as sculpture in antiquity or painting in modern times. They invented an exemplary form of art, addressing themselves to a limited number of readers and working in a small format. Not satisfied with literal illustration of the texts, they constructed compositions which, for all their small dimensions, were as rich in complexity and as perfect as the great ensembles in mosaic or fresco. What they created was a major art, as easel painting, however small in size, was later to become. In time, the art of miniatures, whose highest achievements spread over at least seven centuries, became more diversified, ranging from literal commentary on a text to virtually independent compositions. Like mosaic, the Carolingian miniature came to 14 constitute one of the summits of pictorial art.

And yet this is not the whole story. Miniature painting was not the only form of art in the Western Middle Ages. Very soon Western clerics, reluctant to settle for the snugness of their monasteries and not overly enchanted by the hermit's life, joined in the efforts of cultured, politically minded laymen: they quit their confining walls to win over and organize the populace, at least to the extent the secular authorities had done. From this stemmed a reciprocal exchange of influences which transformed the clergy, as well as the masses they were leading toward the City of God by means of their organization of the City of Man. This was not, as later, an equilibrium between two truths, but rather an integration of two orders reflecting a single common source and aspiration. As early as the tenth century, and parallel with the development of the refined art of the miniaturist, a popular, folk-oriented art sprang up on church walls to proclaim the doctrine of faith to the eyes of all. In their graphic approach, expression, linkage of scenes, treatment of space by expansion or concentration— the same system of exploitation of the image to embody basic beliefs held sway in both arts.

In the twelfth century the third phase of this history began and was marked by the development of the fresco and, finally, of the individual picture. Not that there was any break between the painting of the second phase—of the Carolingian Empire and the feudal struggles—and that of the third. Gothic civilization grew out of Romanesque civilization, which itself was an extension of Carolingian culture. Nevertheless, in the fourteenth century the success of a clerical culture, coupled with economic and political advances in the West, created the conditions for a new organization of power. What is more, it suggested to artists and their patrons new subject matter as well as new modes of presentation. Alongside the military powers—that is, the emperors and kings—and the clergy Rome and the proselytizing militia of the Dominicans and Franciscans (the latter quickly brought into line)—a third, secular, power asserted itself: the middle classes, with their strength massed in cities whose fortune depended on theirs. The result: the range broadened in feeling and in subject matter that was open to art. The innovations of the fourteenth century seem, outwardly at least, inconsistent with each other. The preaching of the first Franciscans kindled a blazing mysticism in which for the first time the ancient intimate dialogue of the human soul with the One God of the Gospels was resumed; but at the same time the century expressed heartily its delight in the good things of the earth. Fashions and domestic decoration and the way things should be done became interesting in themselves for the citydwellers who were the new patrons of art. Meanwhile, the militant religious orders implanted their doctrine of the active life, of salvation through practice rather than contemplative illumination. But however diverse its aims, Gothic art was to enjoy great unity for a long time.

What is so interesting in the development of fourteenth-century painting is the question of the real motivations inherent in it which caused artists, during the first twenty years of the following century, to depart from the Giottesque idiom in favor of that developed by Van Eyck, the Master of Flémalle, and the miniaturists of the French court. This has remained one of the obscure points in history because until now no one has approached it objectively. Starting with an incontrovertible fact —that in Florence around 1425 there was a sudden break brought about by Masaccio's personal genius—historians have neglected the study of the art of the preceding century in and for itself. The academic doctrine enthroned in the nineteenth century propounded the absurd notion that Italian painting of the fifteenth and sixteenth centuries was "realistic." It never occurred to those academics that linear perspective is in no way a practical procedure for the "photographic" representation of the external world as it may exist independently of human consciousness. Perspective is, in fact, no more than a clever studio trick making it easy to repeat certain models having high stylistic qualities which do not in any way imply that the models have achieved absolute objectivity. Any and every representation of the universe necessarily is based on a selection of significant elements. Even hypothetically there cannot exist a total vision outside of human perspectives nor outside the perspectives of man at a given stage in his history. One should not confuse the realism—factual but partial—of plastic figuration with another kind of realism (in itself almost inconceivable), that of an art which would make man the equal of the Creator of the universe or, more precisely, which would require of man the capacity to observe reality not only as his own senses grasp it, but also as it must appear to the creatures beyond number which populate or have populated earth and the heavens. Every art is selective. For that reason it is linked to the demands of a particular way of understanding, and of a need for action determined both by the knowledge and by the powers of a particular society at a particular time and in a particular geographical region. And this is precisely why we can look to painting for information about the social world, but not for the immutable secret of the infinite universe.

There was no precise break between the Gothic world and the Renaissance. Masaccio borrowed from his contemporaries the theoretical and imaginative material for his art, and it took a century before the equilibrium of the two worlds was definitively upset. Gothic culture was international, and included both Giotto and Gentile da Fabriano. The art and the culture of fifteenth-century Europe were developed in the workshops connected with the French court and the Burgundian dukes as much as in the *botteghe* of Florence. Beyond question, it was Masaccio and Brunelleschi who introduced those problems which later, at the start of the sixteenth century in the Rome of Leo X, gave rise to a conception of painting destined to remain the absolute standard for generations to come. But it is simply unthinkable that our age, which, as we stated at the outset, has a wider vision of a vaster history, should retain such a standard. Whether we wish to understand better the fragmentary but effective solutions discovered by the Renaissance, or the Gothic origins of those solutions, or the role of the West within a universal context, it is absolutely indispensable that we reconsider the problem of what part was played by the international workshops of the entire fourteenth century. It was those work-shops which brought into being that efficacious though limited culture which conferred on the West, however briefly, the mastery of the globe, although it did not and could not give the assurance of having penetrated the ultimate secrets of the universe. When such a study has been undertaken, it is probable that our present chronological divisions will lose both their meaning and their value and that we shall perceive a new continuity between Middle Ages and Renaissance. This will entail also our giving up, right from the start, our notion that the Western countries, France and Italy above all, constituted separate hubs of civilization linked to each other by no more than sporadic and ephemeral bonds. A finer, more penetrating knowledge of Western painting leads to the conclusion that we must study it as one of the major factors in civilization. As such, it can spread out before our eyes the fundamental customs, traditions, and structures of institutional and speculative thought that united the entire Western world.

Virgin and Child (?) · 3rd century · Fresco · Catacomb of Priscilla, Rome

This fresco in one of the great Roman catacombs was made, beyond doubt, before the recognition of the Church by Constantine. A secret art in a secret place, it was intended not to impress and overwhelm the masses but, instead, to affirm on a wall tomb, above his mortal remains, the faith and hope of a dead Christian —a functional art if there ever was one. Rather than the usual figure of a praying man or woman symbolic of the deceased's personality, often found elsewhere, here we have one of the first images in which Christian art strove to give material form to the Divine; we are at the first step in the creation of a system of new signs and symbols quite unlike anything known before.

An Ancestor of Christ · 4th century · Mosaic · Chapel of St.
Aquilino, San Lorenzo, Milan

This small chapel, entirely decorated with mosaics around A.D.
350, under Constantine III, is one of the first attempts to create a
complete ensemble of symbols summing up Christian doctrine.
No longer concerned merely with the personal bond between the
believer and his God, what is shown here is the intellectual
system on which rests the institution of the Church in relation to
its origins and traditions. Christ is enthroned in the center between Sts. Peter and Paul and surrounded by the Patriarchs,
Apostles, and Martyrs—all the witnesses to His earthly mission.
The two principal currents of Christian iconography are already
laid down here: narrative and symbolism.

Christ in Glory · Early 5th and 8th centuries · Mosaic · Santa Pudenziana, Rome

An old description allows us to date this admirable mosaic in the reign of Pope Innocent I (401–7). It has come down through fifteen centuries in a comparatively satisfactory state of preservation, although when it was restored at the end of the eighth century two of the twelve Apostles and the two edges of the composition were lost. Nevertheless, the work remains perfectly coherent and without serious alterations. We see Christ enthroned surrounded by the Apostles and the allegorical figures of the New Law and the Old (later, these were personified as Church and Synagogue). The inscription DOMINUS CONSERVATOR ECCLESIAE PUDENTIANAE names Christ Himself as patron of the sanctuary, but behind Him there is also a view of the Heavenly Jerusalem with features borrowed from the real city (the Holy Sepulcher and the Church of the Ascension). From Milan to Rome the doctrine of the Latin Fathers of the Church was beginning to be preached in images.

Story of Moses · 5th century · Mosaic · Basilica of Santa Maria Maggiore, Rome

There survive great ensembles of the mosaics with which Pope Sixtus III (432-40) endowed the basilica on the Esquiline hill. Over thirty of the original forty-two mosaics have been preserved. The Marian dogma had been proclaimed by the Council of Ephesus in 431, but here the scenes from the life of the Virgin on the triumphal arch and around the apse are still associated with subjects from the Old and New Testaments, the Apocalypse, and the life of Christ. Abraham, Jacob, Moses, and Joshua serve as witnesses to the Redeemer, but there are no saints, since these mosaics date from before the time when saints were depicted. In this scene of the revolt of the Hebrews against Moses, the technique is pictorial and entirely Occidental in conception. Here narrative was introduced into monumental art, contrary to contemporary practice in Byzantium: in the West, the need of proving was more urgent than the need to dominate.

Sts. Onesiphorus and Porphyrios · 6th century · Mosaic · Church of
Hagios Georgios (St. George), Salonica

Sometime between 306 and 334 the Emperor Galerius constructed a rotunda in close proximity to a triumphal arch at the
entrance to Salonica. Around 390 Theodosius transformed it
into a palace church and had the interior decorated with mosaics
after having surrounded the church with a circular gallery. In the
center of the cupola soars Christ in the company of angels, and
the drum is decorated with figures of saints against a background
of architecture in the Fourth Pompeian style. The niches are
adorned with flowers, fruit, and birds, and the saints are those of
the Eastern Church calendar. The décor is obviously related to
Persian art and to what was later to become the Moslem style. It
is evident that in Salonica in the fifth and sixth centuries there
existed a *koine*, a common mode, in which the forms, however
Hellenistic they might be, were as much dependent on Roman
and Latin developments as on those of the East. It is difficult to
pin down the liturgical significance of the themes in the central
motif: they might represent either the Fountain of Life or ab-
22 stract designs in conformity with the iconoclastic doctrine.

The Good Shepherd · 5th century · Mosaic · Mausoleum of Galla Placidia, Ravenna

Western counterpart to the Church of St. George in Salonica, this delightful monument was probably begun as the Chapel of the Holy Cross for the palace of Constantius III (d. 421). It was completed around 425 by his successors, Honorius (d. 423) and Valentinian III, respectively brother and son of Galla Placidia who, at her death in 450, was without doubt buried with her husband and her brother. The mausoleum is surprisingly well preserved, and even the light still filters through windowpanes of alabaster. Depicted are Christ as the Good Shepherd gathering souls to Him and, in addition, St. Lawrence with the Cross and the Book, the tunic and the keys—once again the two approaches: symbol and figure. Already certain principles were set down here from which Christian iconography was scarcely ever to stray, and these show the role played by the theologians in the programs they worked out and in the church they guided. But however similar in principle such ensembles as this may be with the decorations of Santa Pudenziana in Rome, not only the work but even its underlying spirit are entirely transformed by a different technique, a different style, a different artist, and the demands placed on art by different patrons.

The Baptism of Christ · 5th century · Mosaic · Cupola, Baptistery of the Orthodox, Ravenna

Once more there is an evocation of the universe itself, but here, in line with the function of the edifice, everything centers around the baptism of Jesus. The principal composition, the Baptism, which is entirely in mosaic, fills the cupola and continues down to the level of the walls where there are two more tiers of decoration; the higher of these is sculpted, and recalls the system used in the church of St. George in Salonica but differs by being in relief. The images in the outer circle of the cupola are not figures but thrones and altars. Thus, as in Salonica, symbolic objects rather than human representations are used here, and this reflects the famous dispute over iconoclasm as well as the relationship between Christian art in the East and that of Islam. The individual components of the vocabulary of images were not devised anew for each new work but rather were drawn in each epoch from an ancient repertory as much as they were invented: what counted was the way they were put together, the montage, what we call the structure or composition.

24

The Empress Theodora · 6th century · Mosaic · Church of San Vitale, Ravenna

The mausoleum of Galla Placidia was the work of the nobility, the baptistery that of the clergy. A century later, under Justinian, the church of San Vitale was built through the initiative of the Archbishop Ecclesius (522–32) and his successors Urcinius (533–36) and Victor (538–45), and completed before 547 by Maximinian, whose episcopal throne still survives. Not the least remarkable trait of this décor is the fact that the Empress is placed on an exalted plane with the great Biblical heroes. This is one of the summits of the art of mosaic.

St. Apollinaris and the Transfiguration · 6th century · Mosaic ·
Basilica of Sant'Apollinare in Classe, Ravenna

This church was founded by Archbishop Urcinius (533–36) and
completed before 549 by the wealthy Julianus, both of them
agents of the imperial reconquest of the territory of Ravenna,
local partisans of the policy of imperial unity. They were among
those who, in the provinces, actively aided in Justinian's great
reconsolidation of the Empire, viewing the undertaking not as
an annexation of Italy by Byzantium but, instead, as a revival of
the ancient Roman dignity to be won by force of arms. However,
the mosaic decoration of this church was not completed until
more than a century later, around 675, in the time of the bishop
Reparatus and of Constantine Pogonatos. It is interesting to
compare this apse with the Good Shepherd in the mausoleum
of Galla Placidia (page 23): here, in striving for artistic unity, both
the symbolic and the figurative elements are relegated to less
important parts of the edifice. San Vitale represents a summit
of art, a classical high point, whereas in this church the first
26 warnings of an impending academicism make themselves felt.

One of the Three Magi · Detail of a nave frieze · 6th century ·
Mosaic · Basilica of Sant'Apollinare Nuovo, Ravenna

Erected under Theodoric around 504, the edifice was consecrated
to the Orthodox cult under Bishop Agnello (557–70) and placed
under the patronage of St. Martin *"in-ciel-d'oro."* When, in the
ninth century, the relics belonging to Sant'Apollinare in Classe
were transferred to this church, its name was changed to the
"new" church of St. Apollinaris. The mosaic decoration of the
upper tier dates from the time of Theodoric. The lowest tier was
executed when the church was reconverted to Orthodoxy about
560, except for the Virgin enthroned and the four angels around
her toward whom winds a procession of the three Magi followed
by the Virgin Martyrs.

St. Demetrius between Prefect Leontius and Bishop John · 7th century
Mosaic · Basilica of St. Demetrius, Salonica

To round out the series of representative mosaics, this work of
the seventh century is typical of the moment when imaginative
invention came to a halt. A comparison of the virtually hieratic
style of these figures with those of the Church of St. George in
the same city (see page 22) shows the strength of the local
"School"; it also reveals the variety that is possible in an art like
mosaic in which, with identical means, works as different as those
in Santa Pudenziana in Rome and those in Ravenna could be
created. This tells us much about the basic character of the mosaic
28 art and also how styles tend to end in academicism.

Story of Adam, from the Ashburnham Pentateuch · North Africa or Spain · 6th century · Manuscript illumination · Ms. nouv. acq. lat. 2334, Bibliothèque Nationale, Paris

This precious manuscript reveals the transition from the antique style of miniature painting to the more narrative forms of the Western Middle Ages. The brilliance of the coloring contrasts with the minute detail and complexity of the drawing. The style is no longer based on the reduction of a monumentally conceived composition into a miniature but, instead, on the exploitation of line itself. Such an art was not aimed at impressing multitudes, but rather at speaking to the learned clerk as he pored over the texts. In these crowded scenes from the Pentateuch, one catches glimpses of the daily life of a society concerned with integrating its faith and its behavior into a living whole.

Christil before Pilate, from a Book of Gospels (Codex Rossanensis) ·
6th century · Manuscript illumination · Treasury of the Cathedral, Rossano

The principle adopted for the decoration of this New Testament
manuscript—only the Gospels of Matthew and Mark survive—
differs from that used in the Ashburnham Pentateuch, but the
elements are identical. Richness and brilliance are achieved here
by the purple background, and a series of scenes directly illustrates the text. The approach invented by the artists of the catacombs reappears here in a new form; henceforth it was continual-
ly to interact with that other approach which inspired the great
monumental decorations. The lavishing of purple, a precious and
costly material, on the pages of the manuscript gave it a value to
which the clerics were not indifferent. Such a manuscript represented for the clergy a capital as tangible as, say, real estate,
and it was also deemed fitting that the word of God should be
30 enshrined in such a valuable object.

St. Luke, from the presumed St. Augustine Bible · Roman · 6th century · Manuscript illumination · Ms. 286, Library of Corpus Christi College, Cambridge, England

Pope Gregory the Great sent this manuscript of the Gospels to St. Augustine, his representative in England and missionary bishop at Canterbury. It bears witness to the importance of the transitional period of the sixth century in which, just before the irruption of Islam, the West laid down the bases of its achievement. There existed in the sixth century a Mediterranean civilization which here and there elaborated elements borrowed from pagan tradition to fit the new beliefs. Thus miniatures became a complement to the monumental wall decorations and lavish arts which were by no means confined to Byzantium alone. 31

Ornamental Page, from the Book of Durrow · 7th century ·
Iona (?) · Manuscript illumination · Ms. A.4.5, Trinity College,
Dublin

In the seventh century, while the Mediterranean art centers were
declining, the first important workshops began to appear in
northern Europe. The monasteries on the Irish coasts and in
Northumbria created a purely native style which spread into
western Europe at the time of the great expansion of the monastic
system under St. Columbanus. Much emphasis has been placed
on the integration of Celtic ornamentation into the Irish idiom,
and certainly a page like this cannot be accounted for without
reference to the style of the Celts, especially their metalwork.

St. Matthew, from the Book of Durrow · 7th century · Iona (?) ·
Manuscript illumination · Ms. A.4.5, Trinity College, Dublin

We know that the Irish missionaries wore garments which earned
them the epithet of "the Striped Ones." Most likely, then, their
garments, especially their liturgical vestments, became, as it were,
the badge of their calling, symbolizing it in both color and
design. The figure of St. Matthew here is "realistic": he is depicted as a monk who spreads abroad the sacred message.   33

Symbol of St. Mark, from the Gospels of Echternach · c. 690 ·
Ireland (?) · Manuscript illumination · Ms. lat. 9389, Bibliothèque
Nationale, Paris

Here is another proof of the delicate and flexible relationship
which, in this style, unites the three aspects of an image: linear
drawing, specific content, ulterior meaning. The Evangelist is
presented here not as a man who spreads the Gospel but as a
symbolic animal in line with a tradition dating back to St.
Jerome. The inscription IMAGO LEONIS shows us that for the
miniaturist himself there was a problem in an image not merely
borrowed from life but representative of an object having sym-
34 bolic value.

The Letters XPI, from the Book of Kells · 8th century · Ireland ·
Manuscript illumination · Ms. A.1.6, Trinity College, Dublin

It is on this manuscript that most of the usual definitions of the
Irish style are based. Here, the principle of ambivalence—of interpretation on different levels—gives way to fusion, to integration, to ambiguity as to the exact significance of those interpretations. Tiny realistic scenes, animals, and figures are wound
into the coils of the arabesques. The decorative element pre-
dominates; ornamentation is no longer a material value in itself
that can be likened to an act of devotion on the part of the scribe;
a book is no longer cherished as a repository of the word of God
but is considered an instrument to transmit texts.

GODESCALC *Christ Enthroned*, from the Gospels of Godescalc, made for Charlemagne and his wife Hildegarde · 781–83 · Manuscript illumination · Ms. nouv. acq. lat. 1203, Bibliothèque Nationale, Paris

A new mode, distinct from that of Byzantium, is in formation, often on the same bases but with a changed spirit. The Godescalc Gospels is still a precious object inhabited by the Word, but, at the same time, the enthroned Evangelists are placed in front of cities, and the Fountain of Life underlines the autonomy of the two worlds whose respective mediators are Christ and the Emperor. The play of ambivalences no longer occurs between image and form but between those who, on earth, administer the divine legacy.

The Fountain of Life, from the Gospels of Saint-Médard of Soissons · Palace School (Ada group), beginning of 9th century · Manuscript illumination · Ms. lat. 8850, Bibliothèque Nationale, Paris

Heading the canon tables is a Fountain of Life, as in Godescalc's Gospels, which may well be the first appearance in the West of this Oriental motif. The decoration is related to that in the Church of St. George in Salonica as well as to the mosaic of the Good Shepherd in Ravenna (page 23). A double convention is developing here, one of themes and one of forms; but the play of combinations always reveals an aim distinct from the customary iconographic program. Power and glory, the government of men, or their death and judgment are each set forth in turn, in a precise relationship with the owner of the book. 37

St. Luke, from the Gospels of Saint-Médard of Soissons · Palace School (Ada group), beginning of 9th century · Manuscript illumination · Ms. lat. 8850, Bibliothèque Nationale, Paris

Here the Evangelist is shown presenting his book on the pages of which are written some of the key words of his gospel. In Godescalc's manuscript, as in most books of the Carolingian period, the Evangelist was depicted in the act of writing his text; thus the variation here is not without significance. In the new Carolingian society, the cleric was the scribe, and on him depended the order of the society: he acted and he advised, and was no longer a mere onlooker. But in the monasteries the chief task remained the preservation and dissemination of the sacred legacy on which human order is founded.

St. Luke, from the Gospels of Ebbo · School of Rheims, beginning of 9th century · Manuscript illumination · Ms. 1, Bibliothèque Municipale, Épernay

The St. Luke seen here constitutes a document of the greatest interest for Carolingian graphic art. There are many illustrations in which the image has a cursive character very close to handwriting itself. In this instance that kind of drawing is elevated into a deliberate stylistic procedure. The depiction of the bull is not without humor, and in the treatment of costume the striving for stylistic effect clearly dominates over symbolic intent. The entire picture is conceived no longer as a sign strictly tied to the literal and allegorical meaning of the image but rather as a work of art interesting in and for itself. Carolingian miniature art disposed of many technical and figurative approaches, from which the artists seem quite deliberately to have picked and chosen. 39

The Emperor Lothair, from the Gospels of Lothair · School of Tours, 849–51 · Manuscript illumination · Ms. lat. 266, Bibliothèque Nationale, Paris

This Bible was executed by a certain Sigualis at the order of Lothair. Following the portrait of the Emperor on his throne, there is Christ blessing, as in Godescalc's Gospels, in this case surrounded by the attributes of the Evangelists. Then follow the canon tables and the Gospels, each of which is preceded by a list of chapters framed like the canon tables, by a figure of the Evangelist, and by a full-page initial in gold. Another step has been taken: the earthly Prince takes precedence over the King of Heaven—and this gives us the first portrait in the history of medieval France. As royal power weakened, the royal person was made the more of, however much his rule might be challenged.

Presentation of the Book to the Emperor Charles the Bald, from the
Vivian Bible · Saint-Martin of Tours, or Marmoutiers, 849–51 ·
Manuscript illumination · Ms. lat. 1, Bibliothèque Nationale,
Paris

This manuscript was prepared by order of Count Vivian Abbot
of Saint-Martin in Tours in 845 and of Marmoutiers in 846. In
this miniature—one of the first depictions of such a presentation
ceremony—Vivian is escorted by members of the clergy of his
two abbeys and followed by, we presume, the scribes of this
Bible: Amand, Sigualis, and Agregarius. The celestial powers do
not directly intervene; they look on from the top of the triumphal
arch surmounting the King's throne.

St. Gregory, from a Sacramentary · School of Corbie, end of 9th century · Manuscript illumination · Ms. lat. 1141, Bibliothèque Nationale, Paris

At St. Gregory's feet two scribes rummage in a chest of books. The Saint is enthroned like Christ or the emperor, a fact which tells us that power no longer belongs solely to the Incarnate Word but to learning itself—i.e., to the clergy. It will be noted that the Saint appears to be hidden behind a curtain which one of the clerks lifts to catch a glimpse of the Holy Ghost, and the perspective organization is quite unlike the treatment we have seen heretofore. The sensitive use of color is admirable and the rendering of volumes truly masterly.

The Prayer of Hannah, from the Paris Psalter · Constantinople,
9th century · Manuscript illumination · Ms. gr. 139, Bibliothèque
Nationale, Paris

It is interesting to compare the Carolingian productions in the
ninth century with those from Byzantium. In Byzantium the
conflict with the Iconoclasts—those opposed to depicting Christ
and the highest mysteries—did not end until 843, and the creative
period leading to the Macedonian renaissance was therefore later
than that of the West: between 880 and the beginning of the
tenth century. The first manifestations were mosaics, in particular
the famous ones in Santa Sophia in Constantinople. In addition
there are many manuscripts from this period among which some,
like the well-known Kludhov Psalter, provide a marginal commentary with tiny scenes illustrating and framing the text. The
treatment is entirely different from that used in the Utrecht
Psalter and the Ebbo Gospels (page 39): not linear in approach,
the tiny picturesque episodes are rendered by colored contours. 43

The Prayer of Isaiah, from the Paris Psalter · Constantinople, 9th
century · Manuscript illumination · Ms. gr. 139, Bibliothèque
Nationale, Paris

The Macedonian renaissance drew inspiration from antiquity,
and the West had nothing comparable to show. The two miniatures reproduced here, the *Prayer of Hannah* and the *Prayer of
Isaiah*, have much in common with those in manuscripts of late
antiquity and are remarkable examples of a renaissance in the
strict sense of the term, such as was virtually unknown to the
Western world. They have been included here to show how
pictures can sum up the different human climates in which
artworks are produced. Where Byzantium strove to preserve
and restore the glorious past by maintaining the intellectual and
social framework of the Empire, the West, even when it took up
the concept of empire, based its action on a thoroughgoing
revision of the relationships between men and men, and between
44 men and things.

The Massacre of the Innocents, from the Codex Egberti · Reichenau, 10th century · Manuscript illumination · Codex 24, Municipal Library, Trier

At the end of the tenth century a new renaissance, the Ottonian, brought forth a new style that was first centered in Lorraine. Otto the Great (936–73) was supporting a movement of monastic reform with the aim of creating an entente between Crown and Church against the feudal lords. The state abbeys became the center of a cultural revival inspired by the example of the Carolingian renaissance. The chancellery and scriptoria created a remarkable series of great illuminated manuscripts. No abbey could compete in this with Reichenau on Lake Constance, whose first abbot, Rudmann (972–84), founded a scriptorium in which an individual style developed very rapidly. A famous psalter was illuminated at Reichenau for Egbert, Archbishop of Trier, and a volume of pericopes (passages from the Gospels for various religious feasts) as a gift from two monks of that abbey. It is interesting to note that the weeping women in this *Massacre of the Innocents* are much like those at the funeral pyre of Dido in the Vatican Virgil manuscript from the fourth century. The source is common to both the Paris Psalter and this Codex Egberti. 45

St. Luke, from the Gospel Book of Otto III · Reichenau, c.
1000 · Manuscript illumination · Ms. Clm. 4453, Bayerische
Staatsbibliothek, Munich

Rudmann was succeeded as head of the abbey of Reichenau by
Witigowo (985–97), and it was then that the Ottonian style
reached its height. Specimens from that workshop show once
again that creativity flowers in diversity rather than in unity, and
that the range of means available to artists was greater than that
of the procedures they actually employed. The Evangelist is
enthroned in the empyrean, holding on his lap the Earthly City,
and seated on the Rainbow of the Alliance, triumphant and
prophetic. The image of his thought, that is usually in the form
of the book placed on the Evangelist's lap, bursts forth from his
arms and head. And the kings of the earth are no more than those
of the Bible: warders of the Divine Law.

46

St. Peter Receiving the Keys, from the Pericope of Henry II ·
Reichenau, beginning of 11th century · Manuscript illumination · Ms. Clm. 4452, Bayerische Staatsbibliothek, Munich

The Pericope of Henry II presents evidence as to the aesthetic
treatment of light. Composition and gestures are simplified, all
attention is concentrated on the painting itself. In it there is an
enthusiastic return to the gold backgrounds of Carolingian art,
a concern with the book as a precious object. The juxtaposition
on the deep gold background of light colors in a much simplified
linear setting; the choice of lilac, sea green, sandy yellows, off-
whites; the partition of the background into bands suggestive of
space—all of these factors reveal an exceptionally refined science
of the spatial values inherent in color. 47

St. John, from the so-called Grimbald Gospels · School of Winchester, beginning of 11th century · Manuscript illumination ·
Ms. Add. 34890, British Museum, London

Parallel with the Ottonian renaissance, another center grew up
in the West during the tenth century: England. Thus began a
second brilliant period in miniature art in the wake of the
Carolingian renaissance and reform, and of the seventh- and
eighth-century works in Ireland. In contrast with the School of
Reichenau, composition here is a function of line and arabesque,
even when the coloring becomes iridescent and brilliant. In the
final analysis, the Winchester style is less antique and more
48 Carolingian in flavor than is the Ottonian.

The Nativity, from the Missal of Archbishop Robert · School of Winchester, c. 1008 · Manuscript illumination · Ms. Y.6, Bibliothèque Publique, Rouen

Robert, Archbishop of Canterbury, driven from his see in 1052, fled to Jumièges to live out his last years. It is thought that he brought with him this manuscript and a Pontifical that is also now in Rouen. This composition is interesting because it combines a typically Carolingian framework with a type of spatial organization destined for a remarkable future. The superposition of the two episodes of the narrative and, above all, their respective positions in a hierarchy introduced a tradition which was to continue until the time of Fouquet.   49

The Three Marys at the Sepulcher, from a Pontifical · School of
Winchester (?), c. 971–84 · Manuscript illumination · Ms. 369,
Bibliothèque Publique, Rouen

This miniature, from the second of the two books probably
brought to Jumièges by the exiled archbishop, reveals how the
English style, with its unitary and majestic composition in the
Carolingian spirit, developed toward an attitude closer to actual
visual experience. Following a figurative phase in which the style
stems from an idea, from a thought made visible, there develops
another phase in which the clergy fulfills its missionary function
by addressing the congregation in more familiar language.

The Building of the Tower of Babel, from the Metrical Paraphrase of Pentateuch and Joshua, by Aelfric · 11th century · Manuscript illumination · Cotton Ms. Claud. B. iv, British Museum, London

Here the image directly illustrates the text in hand. The giant Nembroch who builds the tower had to be named to be recognized, but everyone could understand immediately the everyday labor of the masons. We must keep in mind, however, that the ladder and the door had traditional symbolic meanings far beyond their direct representation.

51

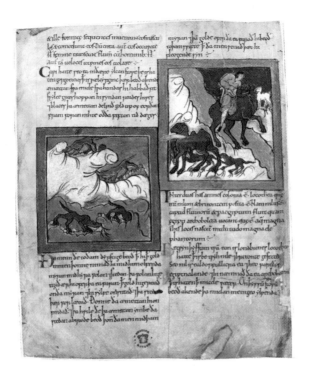

The Land of the Great Ant Hills, from *Marvels of the East* (Astronomical Treatise) · Durham (?), c. 1030 · Manuscript illumination · Cotton Ms. Tib. B. v, British Museum, London

This manuscript, which may be almost contemporary with the preceding ones, testifies to the wide range of culture in England at the close of the early Middle Ages. As is known, there were very few works of secular inspiration, and this account of a voyage is in its way an anticipation of the marvelous tales of Marco Polo as well as of the voyages of Gulliver—an informative document but, at the same time, full of feeling. The linear style is not abandoned but it is combined with other effects, in large part no doubt because the illuminator was working outside of a constraining tradition. Every style implies a certain sacrifice of free invention, and an out-of-the-way manuscript proves that a too perfect style cannot sum up the entire culture in any epoch.

Christ and the Twenty-four Elders, from the Apocalypse of Beatus ·
Saint-Sever (Gascony), between 1028 and 1072 · Manuscript
illumination · Ms. lat. 8878, Bibliothèque Nationale, Paris

The choice of this double plate aims at showing two stylistic
factors: how the rules for dividing the illustrated surface carry
across centuries and schools but do not, for all that, determine
the spirit and character of the image; and how iconography was
revitalized in the eleventh century. Here the eternal problem
of the proportioning of powers between Heaven and Earth has
been left behind, and that of the direct manifestation of the
mysteries has been introduced: evidence of a new and more
immediate relationship between clergy and congregation. There
is a striking parallelism between the formulas that are being
elaborated in this manuscript and those which soon prevailed in
monumental sculpture: artists express in any medium the deepest
significances of their epochs. It will be noticed that the other
two images reproduced from this manuscript divide the figurative
space according to the narrative, whereas here the single vision
has imposed a spatial unity.

The Woman on the Beast, from the Apocalypse of Beatus · Saint-Sever (Gascony), between 1028 and 1072 · Manuscript illumination · Ms. lat. 8878, Bibliothèque Nationale, Paris

The illuminations in this manuscript are particularly numerous and are intended to illustrate the text in detail as it unfolds. To say that this style is popular or folklike would be as inexact as in the case of the manuscript of Aelfric (page 51). Once again we are faced with opposing conceptions in miniature art, paraphrase as against symbolism; and these are the eternal alternatives of all art throughout the ages. The book itself is of very high intellectual quality; this Commentary on the Apocalypse was neither first conceived nor written at Saint-Sever, however: the monk Beatus died in the monastery of Liebana in Spain around 798, and many illustrated versions of his work were made.

The War of the Angels, from the Apocalypse of Beatus · Saint-Sever (Gascony), between 1028 and 1072 · Manuscript illumination · Ms. lat. 8878, Bibliothèque Nationale, Paris

In a series of images the painter laid out the various events of the War in Heaven: first the encounter and what ensued, then, with victory won, the Beast and one of its symbolic allies imprisoned in Hell. The war of the angels is less realistic, but the Beast and the Fallen Souls are depicted with immediacy and are not confined within the dividing bands. The insertion of a second division, the circle surrounded by stars, juxtaposes opposing worlds—Heaven, Earth, and Hell—and the presentation of the Just Soul emphasizes that opposition. There is as much skill in these methods of partitioning space as there was in the treatment of light by the artists of Reichenau, or in the linear approach of Winchester.

The Earth · Detail from an Exultet Roll · Bari, 11th century ·
Manuscript illumination · Archives of the Cathedral, Bari

For the eleventh century there was a real and important problem
involved in the transformation of the spoken sign into a visual
sign, that is, word into image. This is well exemplified in certain
scrolls in southern Italy in which a number of scenes are arranged
one above the other, each illustrating a text which is upside down
in relation to the image. The present picture explains this odd
procedure. It refers to the morning of Holy Saturday at the
moment of benediction of the Paschal candle; from the pulpit the
deacon intones the hymn *Exultet jam angelica turba coelorum*, holding
in both hands the scroll which he unrolls before the congregation.
Thus the faithful can look at the pictures right side up, while the
deacon reads aloud his text with its musical neumes. We see
here that images were presented differently when they were
intended to be looked at by the crowd of the faithful, and when
they were meant to be studied in the silence of the cloister.

The Conquest of England by the Normans: Death of the Brothers of King Harold · Detail from the Bayeux Tapestry · Caen, c. 1070 · Treasury of the Cathedral, Bayeux

It is incorrect to present, as is usually done, the Exultet rolls as isolated examples of the major problem in the early Romanesque period: the new relationship between text and image. The celebrated embroidery presumed to be by Queen Mathilda recounts in more than sixty episodes the expedition across the Channel by William the Conqueror and his victory over Harold. In contrast to the Bari Exultet roll, this text serves only to comment upon or, more precisely, to corroborate the image; the reversal of functions is also contrary to the practice in previous periods, when it was the task of artists to comment on the text, to give material form to the Word. Here is proof of a change in the forms of culture in the Western world occurring between the tenth and the twelfth century, a change much like the one we are experiencing today.   57

The Fall of Man, from an Octateuch · Byzantine, 12th century·
Manuscript illumination · Cod. 8, Topkapi Palace Museum,
Istanbul

A second example of a friezelike composition, here used to
separate the episodes of a narrative, is furnished by this manuscript
typical of the last phase of the Macedonian renaissance. It is the
more interesting in that, for once, we find in the East a remi-
niscence, faint as it may be, of a Western work. In two copies of
the so-called Moutier-Granval Bible the story of the Original
Sin is recounted in very similar fashion: the same principle of
representing figures, the same partitioning, the same rhythmic
scansion of the trees. Since this procedure is also found in
many Romanesque frescoes, no doubt there existed "models"
which circulated throughout the Eastern and Western regions
of the Mediterranean basin. This present example is not a development of the picturesque popular style of the Byzantine
monastery workshops but an instance in a sequence that goes
back to a conservative pictorial tradition.

The Entry of Christ into Jerusalem · School of Monte Cassino, c. 1060 · Fresco · Basilica, Sant'Angelo in Formis (Capua)

Space prevents reproducing here the many works of the ninth and tenth centuries which, in mural art as in manuscript illumination, helped to maintain a tradition common to Byzantium and the Roman and Carolingian West. In fresco painting the dialogue between East and West went on, and the interplay of influences never permits us to define the particular schools with exactitude, but only to detect their traces within individual works. The Romanesque fresco—the next great step in the history of medieval painting after the mosaic—did not constitute a closed world. At the same time that the first Roman workshops were becoming active, this particularly significant cycle was painted in Sant'Angelo in Formis. A little later, around 1070, Desiderius, the great abbot of Monte Cassino, was to call in other artists from Constantinople. All of this suggests the high diversification of art at this time. Furthermore, parallel influences from southern Italy can also be seen. The situation can be summed up as being less a question of Western versions of Byzantine prototypes than of eclectic, international workshops which, each in its way, perpetuated the various styles prevailing at the end of antiquity. 59

Christic the King Enthroned in the Heavenly City · Lombard school,
end of 11th century · Fresco · Sanctuary of San Pietro al Monte,
Civate (Como)

The date of these frescoes is much debated, and some place them
as late as mid-twelfth century. Since the style is traditional, the
problem is of secondary importance. What counts is that here, as
in Sant'Angelo (preceding plate) and at Saint-Savin (pages 64–66),
an entire church has been decorated with frescoes. In content,
they bring together the grandiose apocalyptic vision and the
paradisiac City of God according to St. Augustine. Many elements recall themes and solutions used in miniatures: among the
other frescoes in the church are the Rivers of Paradise and the
Combat of the Archangel Michael with the Dragon. One cannot
simply ascribe these works to Byzantine influence. From one
workshop to another the proportion of such influences varied.
Here the problem of the treatment of depth resembles that in the
St. Gregory of the Corbie Sacramentary and in the presentation
scene in the Vivian Bible (page 41) rather than that in Eastern
60 mosaics.

The Prophet Jeremiah · Lombard school, 1007 (?) · Fresco · Church of San Vincenzo, Galliano (Cantù)

From the point of view indicated in the preceding comment, this fresco cycle from the region of Lake Como is particularly interesting. The church was consecrated in 1007 by a cleric, Ariberto d'Intimiano, who became Archbishop of Milan in 1018 and whose likeness is now in the Ambrosiana in Milan. In the apse there is a theophany, an apparition of Christ: Christ standing, Roman fashion, appears to the prophets Jeremiah and Ezekiel. With its mixture of Roman and Biblical iconographies, was its model Byzantine Greek or Palestinian Paleo-Christian? Below the theophany are several scenes from the life of St. Vincenzo, the patron saint of the church: a hagiographic cycle replacing the traditional evangelical series. All this contributes to the great interest of this ensemble and makes it a good example of the new values coming in at that time. Moreover, one can make out several hands at work in the painting with differences in workmanship, and the personalities of the various artists constitute a point of interest that takes us beyond the conventions that they hold in common.

The Annunciation of Ustyug · Detail of an icon · Novgorod workshop, beginning of 12th century · Tempera on wood · 93¾ × 66½″ · Tretyakov Gallery, Moscow

This famous painting is one of the few surviving from the first period of Russian culture. The standing angel stretches his hand toward the Virgin who stands on a podium and who has an unusual iconographic note: in her breast is seen a haloed image of the Child to be born to her. Above, a mandorla, now mutilated, contains the enthroned Christ. The angel's head has much character in both its features and its plastic treatment. The Byzantine hieratic quality is softened by a sentiment closer to that of the women represented in the Nea Moni in Chios than to that of the workshops in Constantinople.

Adam Naming the Animals · Umbrian school, end of 12th century · Fresco · Abbey of San Pietro, Ferentillo (Terni)

Along with Lombardy, central Italy in the twelfth century was the stronghold of a conservative tradition. In those regions can also be found the link between monumental fresco art and Gothic tapestry. In compositions such as this, one finds reminiscences not only of mural painting of the preceding centuries, but also of certain series of miniatures related to those in the Apocalypse of Saint-Sever (pages 53–55). The fact that, at this date, the figures are still disposed somewhat pell-mell against the background contrasts with the effort made elsewhere—in France and Spain notably—to bring order into the monumental ensembles. This is one reason why Romanesque mural painting is best studied in examples from France.

The Prayer of Enoch · c. 1100 (?) · Fresco · Nave vault, Abbey
Church, Saint-Savin (Vienne)

Founded in the ninth century and rebuilt by the abbot Eudes who
died about 1050, the church was embellished with frescoes apparently in the last years of the eleventh and the first years of the
twelfth century. The decoration covers the crypt, the vault of the
nave, the choir, the bell-steeple porch, and the gallery. The
iconographic program is of unrivaled richness.

The Building of the Tower of Babel · c. 1100 (?) · Fresco · Nave vault, Abbey Church, Saint-Savin (Vienne)

It is impossible to describe adequately the tremendous effort which went into the decoration of Saint-Savin. Begun in part even before the building was finished, the frescoes were carried on concurrently with the construction. Nowhere else is image more intimately linked to architecture: painting here brings the stones themselves to life. Men strove to make this entire monument into an object both precious and replete with life, very much as the Irish miniaturists conceived the Book to be a living treasure incarnating the word of God. But it is the style which is especially outstanding: the figures are at the same time stylized and animated; their liveliness is achieved without any attempt at realism; they are the visualization of thought in action. Moreover, there is perfect equilibrium between what might be called the rhetoric of the forms and the purely plastic quality of the ensemble.

Noah's Ark · c. 1100 (?) · Fresco · Nave vault, Abbey Church, Saint-Savin (Vienne)

We cannot here go into one of the most interesting problems Saint-Savin presents, that of the order in which the frescoes of the vault were meant to be read. The barrel vault was originally intended to be smooth, without transverse ribs after the third span, for the distance that was needed to recount the New Testament stories. However, this plan was abandoned, together with the larger project of decorating the whole church like a kind of jewel box, as in the Orient. Instead, decoration was concentrated at key points; but this made it impossible to unfold a great narrative across an entire wall. This architectonic problem explains why sculpture and miniature eventually supplanted fresco painting. The image reproduced here, if compared with such contemporary works as the capitals in the Church of La Daurade in Toulouse, reveals that all share a single principle of representation that affects iconography, over-all programs, and 66 choice of techniques.

The Creation of Man and the Temptation · First half of 12th century ·
Fresco, detached from the interior of the Hermitage of Vera
Cruz, Maderuelo (Segovia) · The Prado, Madrid

This is an interesting example of how similar problems may find
entirely distinct solutions: as in Saint-Savin, the problem was to
cover a vault. Here, too, the borrowings from the traditional
repertory of motifs are flagrant, and in this fresco we have a
composition which anticipates the sculptured portals of the
Romanesque. On the other hand, while the style of the figure of
Christ may be related to the figures in Saint-Savin, the Adam and
Eve are wholly Byzantine. Twelfth-century Spain acted as a kind
of divide, a watershed between the world of fully developed
traditional forms and the new world in which Romanesque
formulas were beginning to find existence. This comparison
reveals the degree to which Spanish culture was marked by
contacts not only with Islam but also with the entire eastern
basin of the Mediterranean.

David and Goliath · c. 1123 · Fresco, detached from the interior of the Church of Santa María, Tahull (Lerida) · Catalan Museum of Fine Arts, Barcelona

The frescoes of this little church represent the Mozarabic tradition in its purest form. Only four colors are used: white, black, ocher, and vermilion; to the frescoes in the apse are added blue and orange. An archaic note is provided by the short tunic; the fashion for long garments had set in as far back as the 1090s, and it was promptly adopted in the Saint-Savin frescoes. Figure styles provide a sensitive index to the developing phases of a culture: in Saint-Savin is recorded, in fact, the birth of the great Aquitaine civilization.

Decorative Figure · End of 11th century (?) · Fresco · Crypt,
Church of Saint-Nicolas, Tavant (Indre-et-Loire)

This crypt which is completely covered with frescoes is an
entirely separate construction from the church and was probably
built earlier; the style of the frescoes has much in common with
the Carolingian. Here again is a transitional work in which can
be glimpsed the birth of the Romanesque-Gothic civilization
destined to triumph throughout the Western world. This tiny
crypt combines sculptured capitals with frescoed walls. It is still
conceived as a jewel box covered with illustrations which are
held together less by a narrative thread than by their symbolic
meaning.

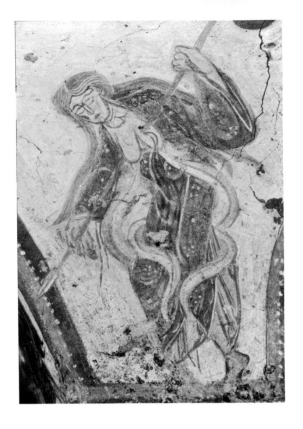

Luxuria · End of 11th century (?) · Fresco · Crypt, Church of
Saint-Nicolas, Tavant (Indre-et-Loire)

The *Decorative Figure* of page 69 and this figure of *Luxuria*
occupy analogous positions on a spandrel of the crypt. Seeing
them side by side emphasizes how innovations may arise within
a system without immediately altering the system as a whole. The
decorative figure suggests in striking fashion not movement as
such (in the sense of the term applied to the Tahull frescoes or to
Carolingian art), but the animation of the personage depicted;
this generates a movement which, being no longer the direct
object of attention, may consequently be most faithfully expressed
by entirely unrealistic methods.

Martyrdom of St. Vincent · c. 1100–1109 (?) · Fresco · Apse wall of upper chapel, Castle of the Monks, Berzé-la-Ville (Saône-et-Loire)

The frescoes in this little Cluniac priory present another problem in the relations between western France and Byzantium: influence from Monte Cassino? from the Ottonians? was a lectionary of Cluny used as model? Together with a great Christ in Majesty in the half-dome of the apse, there are numerous Western saints. The organization of the subject matter is not too unlike that at Tavant or Saint-Savin, but the treatment is quite different. Furthermore, the fresco technique here is not the same as that used in western France: it is instead in the Greek manner with multiple coats of paint.

Virgin in Majesty · End of 12th century · Fresco · Apse vault of crypt, Church of Notre-Dame, Montmorillon (Vienne)

In this church, which belonged to the diocese of Saint-Savin, one sees how, within a century, a compromise took place in the Romanesque style on the eve of a new inspiration, Gothic stained glass. Here we are not far from the first Sienese Madonnas. The Virgin kisses the Child's hand while He places His other on the crowned head of one of the six female saints flanking the mandorla, witnesses to His triumph.

A Saint · End of 12th century · Fresco · Apse vault of crypt, Church of Notre-Dame, Montmorillon (Vienne)

The group of six female saints who flank the Virgin in majesty had many predecessors, notably at Notre-Dame-la-Grande at Poitiers and Castel Sant'Elia near Viterbo. The garments of the saints with their long trailing sleeves date them at the end of the twelfth century. However, the colors—ocher, green, violet—and, even more, the backgrounds with alternating bands of white and gray-blue belong to the Romanesque spectrum rather than the Gothic. Just as the Elders of the Apocalypse are associated in this church with the female saints, so the two styles also intermingle. This figure of a saint is an offspring of the images at Tavant. But, throughout, there is more skill than invention: enthusiastic imagination gives way to elegant reserve. By rejecting nothing, an art always becomes perfected—and impoverished.

Martyrdom of St. James · End of 12th century · Fresco · Saint-Jacques-des-Guérets (Loir-et-Cher)

This church belonged to the abbey of Saint-Georges-du-Bois (Sarthe), held by the regular canons of St. Augustine. The original decoration must quickly have seemed out-of-date, for it was covered over with new frescoes during the thirteenth century. The Massacre of the Innocents, the Nativity, Crucifixion, Christ in Glory, Sts. George and Augustine, Paradise, Pride and Wrath —here we are far from the orderly program of Saint-Savin: the Gothic with its *Summae* of all knowledge has set in, the Romanesque having given up any attempt at system in its ensembles.

St. Paul and the Viper · End of 12th century · Fresco · Chapel of St. Anselm, Christ Church Cathedral, Canterbury (Kent)

Only two chapels in this cathedral have preserved their twelfth-century frescoes, the chapel of St. Andrew from around 1130 and that of St. Anselm from after 1174. In the latter, there remains only the story of St. Paul in Malta (Biblical Melita): while laying sticks on a fire, "there came a viper out of the heat, and fastened on his hand . . . and he shook off the beast into the fire, and felt no harm." The composition is admirable, and there is highly subtle modeling of the face and of the costume which is in the fashion of those at Saint-Savin. The range of colors recalls the Winchester miniatures, and also the frescoes recently discovered in the monastery at Sigena in Spain; however, in either case it would be an oversimplification to speak of Byzantine influence.

Christ Pantocrator between Emperor Constantine IX Monomachus and Empress Zoë · 1028–42 · Mosaic · South gallery, Hagia Sophia, Constantinople

After the Iconoclastic opposition was put down in 843, many sovereigns were depicted rendering homage to Christ or the Virgin, and by the eleventh century the formula had become stereotyped. Byzantium remained faithful to the mosaic technique, while the West preferred frescoes and probably not merely for reasons of economy. I have already stressed the gradual weakening in the West of the concept of the artwork as a rare and precious object in favor of an approach which exploited the images as a free commentary. Doubtless at the start the hieratic character of these images was linked in the East to a certain striving for dignity, like the Roman ideal of impassivity in representing magistrates; but it also soon became no more than a rigid sign, a fixed motif, in consequence of the history of the Eastern Empire.

Virgin and Child between Emperor John II Comnenos and Empress Irene · c. 1118 · Mosaic · South gallery, Hagia Sophia, Constantinople

In this mosaic the head of the Emperor was changed three times—proof of the functional character of this art. The vestments with their liturgical significance came to be more important than the personages they clothed. Moreover, from one section of the mosaic to the next the manner becomes more arid and hard. Only the head of the Virgin was treated with some originality. These were official portraits, and it would be wrong to judge an age only by the portraits and devotional imagery it produced. But the portraits are nevertheless real, while the figure of the Virgin, for all that it is of finer quality, is an icon. Stylistic invention and the technique of execution are at odds here. 77

St. John the Baptist · End of 12th century · Mosaic · South gallery, Hagia Sophia, Constantinople

This beautiful mosaic is part of a *Deēsis:* Christ stands in the center flanked by the Virgin and St. John, a curious iconography implying a kind of synthesis of the themes of the Pantocrator and the Pietà. The pictorial technique here stands out in contrast to the linear stylization which was to become traditional in the Eastern world. In any event, there seems to have been no direct influence from the West. Instead, this work seems to reveal the possibilities that mosaic still offered to artisans of admirable sensitivity although the restrictions of a stereotyped iconography forced their art into academicism.

St. Justus (detail) · Constantinople workshop (?), end of 11th century · Painting on silk · Cathedral of San Giusto, Trieste

To permit a more precise comparison between the different forms of influence—or, better, of relationships—between the West and Byzantium in the eleventh and twelfth centuries, here is a detail of a full-length figure of a saint. His name is written on both sides of his halo in Latin characters, but the style recalls the Byzantine ivories of the so-called Court School. It is interesting that while certain effects of modeling, notably the relationship between the light and heavy parts of the costume, recall the technique of the Canterbury *St. Paul* (page 75), on the other hand everything in the general attitude and facial expression here is totally different from the Canterbury painting.

79

Virgin and Child (Theotokos) · 12th century · Mosaic · Cathedral,
Torcello

Built on the island of Torcello in the Venetian lagoon, the
basilica of Torcello was first decorated with frescoed figures of
saints of which the few traces discovered are markedly Byzantine
in style. Later, in the twelfth century, the decoration was
transformed into mosaic by workshops still Byzantine in tradition
—it was another two centuries before native workshops developed
in the area. The figure of the Virgin is unforgettable, a completely
personal creation in contrast with the other, doubtless almost
contemporary, mosaic on the west wall of the basilica, a Last
Judgment whose crowded folklike character is, to say the least,
lively and amusing. The Last Judgment is a work of folk imagery,
but the great Virgin of Torcello is one of the summits of mosaic
art. For my part, I do not think this use of empty space to
symbolize the ethereal infinity can be related to anything in
Byzantine style. It must certainly have derived from a profound
understanding of a mystical concept that has here been given
truly inspired form, a form which remained as unique and isolated
as the dramatic art of Chios (see following plate).

The Three Marys at the Foot of the Cross · Detail from a *Crucifixion* · Middle of 12th century · Mosaic · West wall, Church of Nea Moni (the New Monastery), Chios

That the hieratic and increasingly stereotyped character of Byzantine art resulted from intellectual conditions rather than from purely technical or stylistic factors is again confirmed by this fine mosaic which makes an interesting comparison with those in the galleries of Hagia Sophia in Constantinople (pages 76–78). The gold background is archaic, but the feeling expressed must have struck its contemporaries as very modern, so different is it from the *Deēsis* in Hagia Sophia: not intimate emotion but, instead, drama.

Noah Sends the Raven and the Dove Out upon the Waters · 12th century · Mosaic · Narthex, Basilica of San Marco, Venice

Rather than from Torcello, this and the next three examples are chosen from San Marco in Venice where one can follow the development of technique and style. In the twelfth century Byzantine or Byzantine-influenced workshops decorated the small cupolas of the narthex, using illustrations from a sixth-century Greek Bible as their models. What is remarkable here is the perfect equilibrium between narrative content and monumental style. In general, in Byzantine art the small episodes are commentaries on a text. Here, the anecdote is part of a pictorial ensemble, and its meaning is immediately understandable even without the accompanying inscriptions. The markedly linear depiction of the waters is balanced by the massive sculpturesque bulk of the Ark.

The Bringing of the Body of St. Mark to Venice · 12th century ·
Mosaic · Wall, south bay, Basilica of San Marco, Venice

Before achieving an independent style, the Venetian workshops
strove to manifest their personality by an individual approach to
iconography, to subject matter. The legend of St. Mark provided
them with an original theme which they exploited with all the
care necessary in recounting events less universally familiar.
Both the inscription and the image function as commentary on
the legend. Here, the soul of the Saint whose body lies lifeless in
the boat is given material form, guiding the seamen who can
only submit to his will. Over and beyond the story itself, this
picture exemplifies the Venetian boast that Providence had
chosen their city out of all the cities of the eastern Mediterranean,
and above all Alexandria, to receive the body and the patronage
of St. Mark.

The Building of the Tower of Babel · 12th century · Mosaic ·
Narthex, Basilica of San Marco, Venice

It is an interesting fact that different techniques and styles were
practiced in periods that were quite close in time, or even within
the same workshops. This mosaic should be compared with the
English miniature on the same subject (page 51). Once again we
see that one style was popular, folklike, and overtly narrative in
contrast to another which was practiced in the great centers
where scribes prepared fine manuscripts for the clergy: the first
had to do with paraphrases of texts, the second led to imposing
Sacramentaries and Pontificals. In this mosaic, there is evidence
of a narrative tradition both persistent and highly international.

The Banquet of Herod · 14th century · Mosaic · Wall, Baptistery, Basilica of San Marco, Venice

In the course of the fourteenth century, precisely when Italian artists were elsewhere laying down modern principles of figuration which made their way only very slowly to Venice, the mosaic workshops in that city were practicing a style infinitely more Byzantine than that of the twelfth century. Comparison of this mosaic with the frescoes of Cavallini at Assisi or of Giotto— all much earlier in date—shows that the Byzantine style dies slowly, frozen into more and more faithful imitation of old forms and with no real innovations. Another example of a Byzantine style ending in academicism can be found in Constantinople itself, in the decoration of the Kariye Camii.

Christ as the Pantocrator · 1148 · Mosaic · Apse, Cathedral, Cefalù

The Norman kings of Sicily, Roger II in particular, founded and
erected in a very short span of time enormous edifices with
interiors sumptuously decorated with mosaics in the Byzantine
manner. Their taste was highly eclectic, for they were rulers by
virtue of conquest, and not natives of the land they governed.
They built Latin edifices, adorned them in Byzantine fashion, and
covered the ceilings with stalactites as the Moslems did. From this
cultural melting pot was to develop in the next century the
civilization of the Hohenstaufens, a high point in the history of
Western thought. In the cathedral of Cefalù the Byzantine style of
the mosaics is out of keeping with the classical character suggested by the basilican plan of the edifice. The individual components remain pure Byzantine; for my part, however, I feel that
in Cefalù as in Torcello there is an exploitation of surfaces and
volumes—especially evident in the Pantocrator and the Virgin
(the latter recalling that of Torcello)—which aims at an impression
86 of relief and, in fact, at an illusionism alien to the Byzantine spirit.

The Nativity · 1132–40 · Mosaic · Nave wall, Palatine Chapel, Royal Palace, Palermo

Founded by Roger II in 1132 and consecrated in 1140, this chapel has a Latin plan, but its mosaic decoration is more Byzantine than that of the Cathedral built a few years later; especially remarkable is the gallery of the "Fathers of the Church," one of the masterpieces of Byzantine style. Nevertheless, certain elements reflect the adaptation of the cycle to a new architectural setting. A composition such as the *Nativity* deserves separate study in itself. It opens the way to the speculations underlying a large part of medieval painting in Italy. Infinitely rich in iconography, it faces up to what later became a major problem, the co-ordination of spatial and temporal factors. We have become so accustomed to the pictorial conventions devised in the West between the twelfth and fourteenth centuries that it is hard to realize that here we have a true imaginative creation. The admirable unity in the chapel is furthered through the harmony of colors.

GIUNTA PISANO (documented 1236–54) *Crucifix* · Before 1236 ·
37 × 28¼″ · Painted wooden cross from the Church of San
Ranierino, Pisa · National Museum, Pisa

The painted crucifix is a transposition into wood of the Byzantine
reliquaries made in the form of a cross in gold or silver and embellished with enamels depicting Biblical scenes, in which the
relics were enshrined in small decorated receptacles fixed at the
lateral extremities of the cross. These jewel-box-like containers
inspired the earliest form and type of decoration of the squared-
off extremities of thirteenth-century Italian crosses. Here then
is a new genre of art: born out of a need for economy—wood was
less costly than precious metals—the painted crucifix, for all
that the material was less elegant, gave rise to new aesthetic
possibilities and a wider dissemination of works of art.

Virgin and Child · Florentine school, second half of 13th century ·
Tempera on panel · Museo Bandini, Fiesole

This panel may have been part of a larger ensemble. Frontal,
rigid, holding the Child who blesses in the manner of the Greek
rite, the Madonna resembles the Byzantine Virgins of the
Nicopea type who hold the Child in a shield (or in place of a
shield) like the pagan Nikes, the goddesses of Victory. This
Madonna is proof that in the second half of the thirteenth century
Florence had not yet shaken off the Byzantine domination which
had prevailed since the sixth century; and also that Florence was
still far behind Pisa, which had begun to liberate itself two generations earlier, and with a refinement unmatched by any other
city in Italy.

THE MASTER OF THE BARDI ST. FRANCIS *Altarpiece of St. Francis* · c. 1250 (?) · Tempera on panel · 92 × 50″ · Santa Croce, Florence

Here we have the basic type of altarpiece of the period: the vertical component of a painted crucifix has been extended to either side to create, in this case, a long vertical rectangle; the lateral areas thus formed are divided into compartments extending to the top and bottom of the panel; each compartment contains a small scene from the life of the holy personage depicted in the center. Here that personage is St. Francis, the ideal saint of the epoch, who according to the doctrine of his Order was the second incarnation of Christ on earth.

BONAVENTURA BERLINGHIERI (c. 1215–after 1274) *A Miracle of St. Francis* · One scene from an altarpiece of St. Francis · 1235 · Tempera on panel · San Francesco, Pescia

This panel comes from an altarpiece almost identical with that reproduced on the preceding page. By comparing them we can learn what is common to the style and what unique to the individual artist. Taken out of its context, this scene of a miracle of the Saint seems remarkably more advanced in style than those of the Master of the Bardi St. Francis and of the Pisan artist reproduced on the next page; this is not a matter of superior quality but of a different spirit. At this early date this artist has faced problems of perspective which were to be posed again in very similar terms a century later.

ANONYMOUS PISAN PAINTER (MASTER OF THE SAN MATTEO
CRUCIFIX) *Pietà* · Compartment from a painted crucifix · Between 1200 and 1230 · Tempera on parchment, attached to
wood · National Museum, Pisa

This *Pietà* has been chosen because of the extraordinary quality
of its composition, draftsmanship, and coloring; it gives some
idea of the high achievement of Pisan art in the first half of the
92 thirteenth century, a period too often undervalued by historians.

Follower of GUIDO DA SIENA *Altarpiece of St. Peter* · c. 1280 ·
Tempera on panel · 32¼ × 65″ · Pinacoteca Nazionale, Siena

The great altar frontals, such as the one dedicated to Mary
Magdalen now in the Accademia of Florence, were fixed in
place and intended for churches only. For private chapels in
homes or for a usage which consisted of placing the painting
below a table, smaller types were needed like this portable
altarpiece *(paliotto)* dedicated to St. Peter. A seated figure
fits this small format better than a standing one; thus, the saint
enthroned became a feature of portable altars and, eventually,
even of large altar paintings with, naturally, suitable enlargement
of the figure. This St. Peter, still somewhat hieratic in manner,
is surrounded by four episodes from his life that are in much
freer and more animated style, and by two scenes from the life of
the Virgin. The presence of the Virgin suggests that this *paliotto*
was perhaps intended for a private chapel.   93

Eliezer and Rebecca (?), from the Psalter of St. Louis · Parisian
workshop, between 1253 and 1270 · Manuscript illumination ·
Ms. lat. 10525, Bibliothèque Nationale, Paris

This psalter according to the rite of Sainte-Chapelle was executed
for the King and embellished with seventy-eight full-page illuminations on facing pages with the explanatory texts on the blank back
pages. It is worth comparing these admirable compositions with
the contemporary paintings produced in Italy, which are too often
considered without reference to the great currents of European
culture in the period. In the thirteenth century, the great art of
painting was French, which is to say Parisian. Gothic painting is
not best expressed in frescoes but in miniatures and stained glass:
the art is offered on the one hand to the admiration of everyone,
on the other, to the small number of cultured persons, but it is the
same taste which is revealed. Gothic civilization was the great
94 form of medieval art—and its center was north of the Alps.

Abraham and the Three Angels, from the Psalter of St. Louis ·
Parisian workshop, between 1253 and 1270 · Manuscript
illumination · Ms. lat. 10525, Bibliothèque Nationale, Paris

Here is a second example of this admirable art, to stress the
perfect and exceptional harmony in all techniques in this remarkable period of the history of the arts. The impressiveness
of architecture and stained glass was matched by an art of
drawing which went hand in hand with masterful use of color.
The Tree of Life continues the old Romanesque tradition but
also anticipates Piero della Francesca, nor was the still life
mastered by the Italians until the next century. The episodes are
at the same time interrelated and distinct. This painter possessed
an art of figurative exposition never again equaled. Here we have
a marvelous example of a visual culture in full possession of its
own means.

Calendar Frontispiece, from the Psalter of Paris · Parisian workshop, c. 1223 · Manuscript illumination · Ms. 1186, Bibliothèque de l'Arsénal, Paris

Intended for a woman of the royal house, this psalter was also part of the Treasury of the Sainte-Chapelle. It includes a calendar and twenty-five full-page illuminations. Preceding the calendar is this miniature in which we see a scribe, a mathematician, and an astronomer holding an astrolabe: where once had figured the Evangelist—vessel and witness of the Divine Word—now appear scientists who explore the universe. Their learning no doubt has an astrological flavor, but it is no less true that with their eyes fixed on the heavens, in the midst of nature symbolized by the trees, these men confront the precepts of divine science with the data of direct observation.

Coppo di Marcovaldo (documented 1260–85) *Crucifix* · Between 1260 and 1265 · Tempera on panel · 116 × 97″ · Museo Civico, San Gimignano

Among the anonymous artists of the thirteenth century, Coppo is one of the first whose personality can be pinned down. A native Florentine, he took part in the battle of Montaperti, was taken prisoner by the Sienese, and remained for some time in their city where he received certain commissions: a *Madonna Enthroned* for the Servites in Siena, and this *Crucifix* for San Gimignano. Far from attempting to throw off the Byzantine tradition, he revitalized it by a remarkable intensification which contrasts with the earlier stereotyped treatment in Florentine art.

MASTER OF VICO L'ABATE *The Miracle of the Bull*, from the altar
frontal of the Archangel Michael · c. 1260 · Tempera on panel ·
Church of Sant'Angelo, Vico l'Abate, near Florence

The anonymous and perhaps provincial artist who painted this
altar frontal likewise profited from the new Eastern science
favored by Coppo but, less learned and less powerful, he injected
into it naïve and spontaneous accents which lend it a quite special
savor. If in Coppo's *Crucifix* the figure of Christ is already con-
ventionalized, and if what is personal to Coppo is only to be
found in the small panels and the Christ in benediction at the
apex, here the entire painting is more homogeneous and infused
throughout with the same creative vigor evident in the single
panel reproduced. Everything is a pretext for this artist to make
what we call today a "bit of painting": the humorously treated
bull, the thick plant in the foreground (more conspicuous than
the animal around which the story centers), the rock at once both
contorted and smooth, the self-possessed attitudes of the personages, their plump individualized faces.

MELIORE *The Crucifixion of St. Peter with Three Women* · Detail from an altarpiece of the Virgin and Child, flanked by Sts. Peter and Paul · 1271 · Tempera on panel · Church of San Leolino, Panzano (Tuscany)

Quite unlike the Master of Vico l'Abate, the Florentine Meliore, who collaborated with Coppo di Marcovaldo on the great *Last Judgment* of the Baptistery of Florence (see page 105), intensified his expressionism to the point of tragedy: rhythmical figures disproportionately elongated, angels with profoundly intent expressions and cruel mouths. In 1271 he signed the altarpiece of which this panel is a part; its central portion, the enthroned Virgin framed by Sts. Peter and Paul and four small compartments, is still in Panzano near Siena, while the ogive painted with a blessing Christ very much in the latest Byzantine manner is in the Uffizi in Florence.

GUIDO DA SIENA *Virgin in Majesty* · Central panel of an altarpiece · 1262 (?) · Tempera on panel · Palazzo Pubblico, Siena

Guido da Siena, reputed the master and ancestor of the entire Sienese school, is known only through this fine painting restored and repainted in the early fourteenth century by an artist in Duccio's circle, perhaps by Duccio himself. The name of Guido can be read on it along with a date which seems to be 1221: for stylistic reasons and historical probability, it is generally dated around 1262. For the same reasons another Madonna in the Pinacoteca of Siena is attributed to Guido, with the same date, this one cut down to half-length but otherwise better preserved.

Roman Master *The Original Sin: Adam* · c. 1290–95 · Fresco ·
Upper Church, Basilica of San Francesco, Assisi

In the third quarter of the thirteenth century, Florence went
through a Byzantine revival as a result of improved acquaintance
with the art of Crete, the Balkans, and Sicily. Siena in this period
continued to refine on the Byzantine tradition by lending its own
characteristic temperament. Meanwhile, Rome turned back to its
own original fountainhead, ancient art. In Assisi, among the
cohort of painters who rushed in from every artistic center of
Italy, the Romans played an important role, even if they remain
anonymous.

Pietro Cavallini (active c. 1270–1330) *Apostle* · c. 1293 ·
Fresco · Church of Santa Cecilia in Trastevere, Rome

This figure is one of tne twelve Apostles who, with the Virgin
and St. John the Baptist, surround Christ in the Last Judgment,
the surviving section of what was once an extensive decoration.
Attributed by Lorenzo Ghiberti, along with the rest of the
decoration, to Cavallini, whose native origins are not known, this
figure is less supple than those by the Roman painters at Assisi;
but in compensation it displays a robustness which, at that
period, could only come from contact—direct or indirect—with
the art of antiquity.

The Twenty-four Elders of the Apocalypse · c. 1255 · Fresco · Apse of crypt, Cathedral, Anagni

Along with Assisi and Rome, Anagni—a city made notorious a little later by the attempt against Pope Boniface VIII committed in the name of Philip the Fair—offers another example of great mural decoration in Italy at the time when France was developing the art of stained glass. It is also one of the last examples of extensive mural decoration in the spirit of the old traditional style and iconography; soon, with Giotto, there was to be more stress on narrative. Here, in this monumental cycle commemorating the dedication of the church and the acquisition of its relics, we find an ultimate summation. It shows man the microcosm in his mystical relations with the destinies of the universe, the same comprehensive program found on the great Romanesque portals such as Beaulieu and Saint-Denis. Painting is still concerned with cosmic symbols; later it was to give concrete form to legends. The saints and the deeds of mankind were more and more to interpose themselves between God and man.

Jacopo Torriti (or da Torrita) *The Coronation of the Virgin* ·
1295 · Mosaic · Main apse, Basilica of Santa Maria Maggiore,
Rome

The signature and date on this mosaic are the only documents
we possess for this artist except for the signature placed in 1291
on the apse mosaic in San Giovanni Laterano, Rome; the latter
mosaic, entirely remade, can no longer tell us anything about
his way of working. Today it is thought that he was perhaps
responsible for certain of the frescoes in Roman style in Assisi
but that, in any event, he started out like Cavallini by restoring
fifth-century Roman frescoes and gained from them his knowledge
of an art still inspired by antiquity. This *Coronation*, like other
thirteenth-century mosaics, strives to respect the style—realistic
and adopting small scenes in the open air—still visible in certain
vestiges of fifth-century decoration which remained in place and
are not greatly removed from the style of Pompeii.

Last Judgment · End of 13th century · Mosaic · Cupola, Baptistery of San Giovanni, Florence

This great work was conceived, as in Byzantine churches, as a veritable microcosm in which a celestial hierarchy presides over Genesis, the Passion, events from the Old and New Testaments, and finally an overwhelming Last Judgment; it was certainly made by a team of artists, not by one man alone. In this universe swarming with details, placed too high to be easily analyzed, the center of interest is the Christ of Judgment enthroned in glory on the rainbow of the Apocalypse and, with a broad gesture, separating the Good from the Bad among the resurrected dead at His feet. The figure has often been attributed to Cimabue, but Carlo Ragghianti's suggestion of Coppo di Marcovaldo, probably assisted by Meliore, seems quite valid. To whomever the mosaics in the Baptistery of Florence may be due, one can say without hesitation that they belong to a current opposed to that of the apse mosaic of Santa Maria Maggiore in Rome: they are Byzantine and in no way Roman.

CIMABUE (CENNI DI PEPO) (1240/50–1302/3) *Crucifix* · Before
1270 (?) · Tempera on wood · 11′ × 8′11″ · Church of San
Domenico, Arezzo

While the collaboration of Cimabue in the Baptistery of Florence
is no more than a probability, there is general agreement in
attributing to him this *Crucifix* which he would have painted at a
time when he was still much involved in the Byzantine current
of Coppo. In any event, his affinities with Coppo, whose work
was always a little cold and formal, are limited to the technical
conception. Even in such youthful efforts, Cimabue was
concerned above all with expression, seeking to reveal in both
human figures and objects the dominant and single idea behind
them. Among all the Christs of the epoch, those of Cimabue are
the supreme example of the Christ who suffers beyond death
itself.

CIMABUE *Virgin and Child with Angels and St. Francis* · 1282–1301 ·
Fresco · Lower Church, Basilica of San Francesco, Assisi

It was Vasari who first attached the name of Cimabue to this
fresco which Ghiberti had given to Cavallini; today, opinion
unanimously assigns it to Cimabue. If there has been uncertainty,
it was because the gap between the two artists tended to lessen
in the period of Cimabue's maturity when he increasingly
abandoned Byzantine formalism in favor of greater freedom in
the means of expression. Those means were adapted with remarkable consistency to the artist's fundamental concern with
bringing out the chief emotional and ideological characteristics
of his personages: here the Virgin is doubly maternal, mother
not only to the divine Infant but also to the humble and human
St. Francis, the second incarnation of Jesus. The soft coloring
and the velvety treatment of what already deserves the name of
chiaroscuro aid alike in softening an implacable divinity in favor
of a more human truth.

CIMABUE *St. Luke* 1282–1301 · Fresco · Crossing, Upper Church, Basilica of San Francesco, Assisi

For the four sections of the cupola, placed very high, each of which is devoted to one of the Evangelists, Cimabue went back to a linear treatment more easily decipherable at a great distance; he also reverts a conception of space which, without imitating that of the Romans, no less clearly renders the three dimensions of the cities over which reign Luke, Matthew, Mark, and John, each of them identified by a legible inscription as well as by his small conventional symbol. The large city which supersedes the symbol was an innovation in monumental art and must certainly have derived from manuscript illuminations whose style, more-over, is imitated here.

GIOTTO DI BONDONE (c. 1266–1337) *The Stigmatization of St. Francis* · c. 1296–1304 · Fresco · Upper Church, Basilica of San Francesco, Assisi

Giotto went to Assisi at the invitation of Giovanni di Muro, general of the Franciscan order between 1296 and 1304. So it is probably between those dates, most likely about 1297, that the artist's arrival in the city of St. Francis took place, although he seems to have visited it about 1295. It is now generally agreed that it was in fact Giotto, no doubt with the aid of a large group of students, who during his second sojourn in the city executed the twenty-eight frescoes in the Upper Church which illustrate the life of St. Francis. Before Giotto there had been numerous interpretations, painted and written, of the legend of the Saint; Giotto gives us a conception that is ideologically official, but artistically very new. This and the following example, the *Confirmation*, have been chosen because they demonstrate better than the other frescoes the synthesis of these two normally contradictory aspects in this complex work.

GIOTTO DI BONDONE *The Confirmation of the Franciscan Rule by Pope Honorius III* · c. 1296–1304 · Fresco · Upper Church, Basilica of San Francesco, Assisi

Like the *Stigmatization*, this fresco was conceived to assert to the world the rank of St. Francis in the hierarchy—in this case, on earth; in the preceding example, in Heaven. The stigmata received by the Saint are the proof that he relived on earth the same existence as Christ and that he is therefore, after Christ, the most important personage in the universe. Both of these works, especially in the treatment of the draped figure as inspired by French and Pisan sculpture, constitute a breakthrough to a new art destined to depart from the established tradition, an art of which Giotto himself in his subsequent works was to be the principal agent.

GIOTTO DI BONDONE *The Dream of Joachim* · 1304–5 · Fresco ·
Scrovegni Chapel, Padua

Even more than at Assisi, the sculptural quality of Giotto's
figures is evident in his frescoes for the chapel of Enrico Scrovegni, known as the Arena Chapel because it was built on the
ruins of an ancient amphitheater. Enveloped—shrouded, rather,
in a manner that makes us think of French funeral monuments—
in the ample folds of a cloak with broadly modeled surfaces, the
figure of Joachim sleeping is like a block of stone, compact,
scarcely altered by the sculptor's tools, much like the statues of
Giovanni Pisano who, as it happened, was himself at Giotto's side
during the work on the chapel. The few years between the
Assisi frescoes and those at Padua have sufficed not only to ripen
Giotto's talent but also to make him conscious of the path his
quest had to pursue.

GIOTTO DI BONDONE *The Presentation of the Virgin in the Temple* ·
1304–5 · Scrovegni Chapel, Padua

The progression of any development is always partial. If at times
Giotto concentrated entirely on the human figure, at others he
continued to include, unmodified, many elements of setting
belonging to the authentic Byzantine repertory of images and in
particular to that of Sicily: the imaginary stylized rock of *The
Dream of Joachim*; the small marble edifice, scarcely more than a
shell, with its slender columns, which represents here the Temple;
still others which set the stage for most of his narrative scenes.
As a matter of fact, the juxtaposition of the two approaches
enhances the effect, as here where the fragility of the architectural
setting only makes the natural weight of the human figure so
much more evident. There is one true invention here, however,
in the depiction of architecture: the bare steps of the staircase,
with all their solidity, on which poises the tiny figure of Mary—
the motif was to survive and to be repeated with great effect as
late as Titian and Tintoretto.

GIOTTO DI BONDONE *The Entry into Jerusalem* · 1304–5 · Fresco ·
Scrovegni Chapel, Padua

The Entry into Jerusalem is a subject that has much to offer the
painter. It requires a variety of picturesque elements which blend
nicely: a city or its gate, a procession and a counterprocession,
a cloak spread out, trees, a donkey. For this reason the subject
had been popular since early times, and all its elements had
become virtually obligatory, fixed by a long-standing tradition.
Giotto kept them all, but far from aiming at merely picturesque
effect, as Duccio did in the same subject painted at the same time,
Giotto condensed the conventional elements to the minimum
and treated them as simple signs, mere indications: the city gate
is barely visible in the corner, the boys gathering palm branches
are relegated to the background, the two processions do not
straggle off into space, the cloak covers no more than a bit of
the path. All interest is focused on the majestic figure of Christ
and on His mount and, above all, on the dramatic encounter.

GIOTTO DI BONDONE *The Kiss of Judas* · 1304–5 · Fresco · Scrovegni Chapel, Padua

It is in this masterly fresco that Giotto reveals the full measure of his quintessential humanism. The fraction of space left unfilled by figures is animated only by the lances and blazing torches which are dependent on the hands that hold them. There is a single plastic motif: the bringing into relief of the principal figures in the compact crowd. There is also a single emotional motif: the contrasts between the falsely fraternal gesture of Judas, Jesus' awareness of it that is expressed in His face, the panic of the Apostles, and the vulgar brutality of the myrmidons of the law eager for their prey.

GIOTTO DI BONDONE *Last Judgment* · 1305 or 1306 · Fresco ·
Scrovegni Chapel, Padua

Giotto culminated his work with this *Last Judgment*, which
stretches across the entire entrance wall of the chapel. Crowning
all, Paradise; in the center, the Christ of Judgment and a row of
Apostles; below, the Elect and the Damned. The over-all plan
of the fresco is of special interest for its perspective treatment of
the fan-shaped ranks of haloed angels' heads on either side of the
window, and also for the architectural *trompe l'oeil* separation of
Heaven and Earth, the first of a long series of such illusionary
renderings in the decoration of large wall surfaces.

GIOTTO DI BONDONE *The Burial of St. Francis* · Between 1317 and 1320 · Fresco · Bardi Chapel, Basilica of Santa Croce, Florence

Established in Florence, famous, wealthy, and admired, Giotto received many commissions to decorate the private chapels the greatest families of Florence were privileged to set up in the transept of Santa Croce, which was, along with the Dominicans' Santa Maria Novella, the most important church of the city and the official seat of monastic and papal Franciscanism. Four of these were decorated by Giotto's workshop: the Bardi, Peruzzi, Giugni, and Tosinghi chapels, but only the frescoes of the first two have survived; completely whitewashed over, they were not discovered until 1841. Very much restored since, they still have much to tell us, if only about the choice of subjects and the ultra-official type of composition in favor at the time. The frescoes constitute, in fact, an apologia for Franciscanism, which had made its peace with the Church of Rome by complete submission. In any case, this burial scene is a masterpiece of composition whose measured rhythm could well be envied by many a great classical artist.

This is not an isolated work but one of a long line of enthroned Madonnas which, no longer of the frontal hieratic type long favored in Byzantine Italy, are in three-quarter profile bending down toward the Infant. All of them are seated on a throne as monumental as a church—this throne is, in fact, a symbol of the Church. But the Madonna of Badia carries over from the past her mantle streaked with gold, the Child who blesses in the Greek fashion, and the two angels who must always, according to the tradition of Constantinople, attend the Virgin.

DUCCIO DI BUONINSEGNA *The Virgin in Majesty* · Central panel
of the front of the Maestà Altarpiece · 1308–11 · Tempera on
panel · 84 × 157″ · Museo dell'Opera del Duomo, Siena

This central panel of the renowned altarpiece from the Siena
Cathedral has a Virgin of the same type seated on a monumental
throne, but she has developed, become more supple, and the
Child has become a believable infant. The Byzantine attributes
have been discarded, although the style remains close to the
Greek. The two angels have increased to twenty, a heavenly
court, and the court is rounded out by ten saints, among whom
are the patron of Siena, St. Catherine, and four saint-protectors
of the city. And yet this Queen in the center of her court, with
the twelve Apostles as guard of honor, is nonetheless a younger
sister to the Madonna at Badia a Isola and to all those preceding
her. The *Maestà* was commissioned from Duccio in 1308 by the
Commune of Siena to be placed in the Cathedral. The day it
was finished, it was borne in triumph to its new home by an
118 ecstatic populace: Duccio's fame was assured.

DUCCIO DI BUONINSEGNA *The Virgin Borne to Her Sepulcher* ·
Superstructure of the Maestà Altarpiece · 1308–11 · Tempera
on panel · 21¾ × 19¾″ · Museo dell'Opera del Duomo, Siena

The life and death of this Queen reigning over a heavenly court
are recounted in six scenes. Such scenes had become virtually
obligatory ever since the early crucifixes and altarpieces of saints
with accessory narrative panels. But in the *Maestà* the expanse
required for the great court—both ideologically and pictorially
an innovation at the time—created a problem: to place the narrative scenes at the sides of these ranks of figures would mean
breaking both the style and the significance of the composition.
Therefore Duccio had the happy thought of placing them all at
the top of the altarpiece to form a large superstructure (which
was later detached from the rest of the painting). This innovation
was later followed only in part: although altarpieces were more
and more given a decorative superstructure, the theme was
generally confined to the Annunciation or to isolated figures
without narrative scenes.

DUCCIO DI BUONINSEGNA *The Apparition of Christ through a Closed Door* · Panel from the back of the Maestà Altarpiece · 1308–11 · Tempera on panel · Museo dell'Opera del Duomo, Siena

Duccio's great altarpiece is unique in that it was meant to be viewed from both front and back. One wonders if the notion may not have come from the famous *Pala d'Oro*, the gold altarpiece in San Marco in Venice, the contacts between Siena and Venice having certainly been more extensive and more frequent at the time than has hitherto been recognized. The back of the *Maestà* is entirely devoted to scenes from the life of Jesus. No attribute sets Him apart from the Apostles, but He is recognizable from one scene to the other by His red robe and blue mantle. However, for the apparitions after the Resurrection, Duccio had recourse to another procedure: the risen Christ is clothed in a gold-streaked mantle in accord with the Byzantine tradition. Thus, to indicate the transformation from the human to the divine, Duccio dipped back into Byzantine art, still considered more noble and, in any case, most effective in representing the extraspatial character of God.

DUCCIO DI BUONINSEGNA *The Flight into Egypt* · Panel from the predella of the Maestà Altarpiece · 1308–11 · Tempera on panel · Museo dell'Opera del Duomo, Siena

The predella—a row of small square or rectangular panels generally of uneven number (three, five, or seven) placed below the central panel of an altarpiece as a sort of dado or pedestal— became the favored location for small narrative scenes. Although Duccio had already made use of the superstructure for these, he also utilized the predella. Small scenes on the predella on the back of the *Maestà* continued the account of the life of Christ, while on the front others, separated by figures of prophets, were devoted to the Virgin. The seventeen panels known to have survived have been dispersed to various museums, but whatever others there were have disappeared. *The Flight into Egypt*, one of seven remaining in Siena, has a picturesque character entirely alien to the severity of the main central panel, although Duccio, unlike other artists, lavished on it the same highly controlled drawing and the same painstaking execution as on the principal section of his altarpiece.

121

Duccio di Buoninsegna *The Entry into Jerusalem* · Panel from
the back of the Maestà Altarpiece · 1308–11 · Tempera on panel ·
Museo dell'Opera del Duomo, Siena

Compared with Giotto's treatment of the same subject (page 113),
this *Entry* employs all those illustrative elements which had
become traditional, but nevertheless reveals that something quite
different could be made out of them. Duccio does not emphasize
the figure of Christ but, instead, the city, the procession, the
landscape, and the spread-out cloak, and he disposes them all in
depth, distributed throughout the various planes, and this well in
advance of any hint of later theories as to how space should be
represented.

DUCCIO DI BUONINSEGNA *Jesus before Annas* and *The First Denial of Peter* · Panel from the back of the Maestà Altarpiece · 1308–11 · Tempera on panel · Museo dell'Opera del Duomo, Siena

Here we have two interiors superimposed. Their cuboid, scenic, and perspective character is perfectly well brought out: note the staircase which carries the eye upward, the arcade below with its glimpse of the entrance, and the ceiling of the upper room. Nevertheless, it may well be that this practice was reserved to minor types of painting, to small scenes, while the "noble" style appropriate to large central panels continued to call for the Byzantine manner.

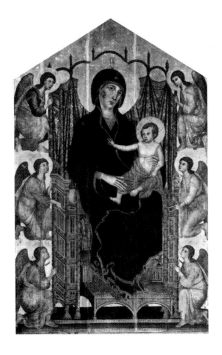

Duccio di Buoninsegna *The Rucellai Madonna* · 1285 (?) ·
Tempera on panel · 14′ 9⅛″ × 9′ 6⅛″ · Uffizi Gallery, Florence

This painting was found in the chapel in Santa Maria Novella
which had belonged to the Rucellai family, and this accounts for
the name currently given to it. One can see how far the painter
had come from the Madonna at Badia a Isola, and how close he
was already to the Virgin in the central panel of the *Maestà:*
the mantle no longer has Byzantine gold streaks to symbolize
folds in the drapery, and those folds are now carefully worked
out for plastic form and suppleness. The angels—of which
Byzantine tradition had always required two—have been
multiplied threefold. The rigid and monumental superstructure
of the throne has been replaced by a curtain falling in draped
folds. The Infant is no longer a tiny adult and, without yet being
truly a baby, is at least a child.

SIMONE MARTINI (c. 1282–1344) *Guidoriccio Ricci da Fogliano* ·
1328 · Fresco · Palazzo Pubblico, Siena

Four years before Duccio's death in 1319, another *Maestà*
adorned the walls of a hall in the palace of the commune, the
work of the young Simone Martini. To have been awarded such
an official commission during Duccio's lifetime, the artist must
already have gained a considerable reputation. His fame grew:
an invitation from the King of Naples, commissions from Pisa
and Orvieto, capped in Siena itself by yet another assignment for
the communal palace, this fresco. Since Duccio's heyday the
world had changed, the barrier separating the realms of East and
West had been crossed. The Western world was the world of the
Crusades, not long past but already legendary. What the city
fathers had in mind was a simple votive painting, a victory
trophy of thanks from the thriving commercial middle-class
city to a captain-at-arms, the *condottiere* Guidoriccio, who had
conquered for it the two castles we see in the fresco. But for this
simple task the artist conceived a veritable poetic incarnation of
the chivalric ideal of the Western Middle Ages—the finest
masterpiece of Sienese painting.

SIMONE MARTINI *St. Martin Renouncing the Sword* · Detail from
the cycle of the Life of St. Martin · 1326–28 or 1328–30 or both
in two separate working periods · Fresco · Lower Church,
Basilica of San Francesco, Assisi

The Assisi frescoes portray the world of chivalry, which was no
longer a reality though it continued to excite the nostalgia of an
artist who, living in the most commercially minded city of Italy,
nevertheless thought of himself as a great gentleman. It seems
likely that he acquired such tastes during his stay at the court of
Robert of Anjou in Naples, because before then he was said to be
sober in manner. His talent was at ease in either attitude, but the
pleasure he took in conjuring up military dress and trappings is
more evident in these frescoes than in works like the polyptychs
for Pisa and Orvieto.

SIMONE MARTINI *The Annunciation* (detail) · 1333 · Tempera on panel · Uffizi Gallery, Florence

This polyptych, dated and signed by both Simone Martini and Lippo Memmi, who probably did the wings, was formerly in the Chapel of St. Ansano in the Siena Cathedral. Was it because it was conceived as an altarpiece, like the polyptych in Pisa, that Simone, who had set his frescoes for Assisi and Siena against a radiant blue sky, settled here for the conventional gold background? Whatever the reason, the background is the only concession to the old Byzantine tradition in the delightful central panel; its fluid and somewhat mannered drawing and its fluttering drapery seem Baroque before the fact. But perhaps there is something Byzantine in Simone's very personal interpretation of the Virgin of the Annunciation as an *ancilla Domini*, as Byzantium considered her to be even after the West had proclaimed her Queen. Surely the artist must have had his own opinion, since his Handmaiden of God is both timid and palpitant with life, and this indeed transcends the tradition of any country, of any time. 127

SIMONE MARTINI *The Way to Calvary* · c. 1342 · Tempera on
panel · 9¾ × 6¼″ · The Louvre, Paris

It is thought that this panel was part of a portable polyptych
which once belonged to Cardinal Stefaneschi. It must have been
done at Avignon, where Simone lived from 1340 until his death
in July, 1344, and where he painted frescoes on the façade of
Notre-Dame-des-Doms, now half ruined. Better than the
damaged frescoes, this panel reveals the hold Provençal art took
on the style of the Sienese master, both in the transformation of
his color, which has become flickering here, and in a certain
jaggedness of line not related to the Gothic art of Flanders and
France.

SIMONE MARTINI (?) *The Blessed Agostino Novello Saves a Child Fallen from Its Cradle* · Panel from a triptych · c. 1330 · Tempera on panel · Church of Sant'Agostino, Siena

Had Simone once before succumbed to the fascinations of the folk style? The large votive painting of the miracles of the Blessed Agostino Novello, a saintly hermit-knight, is not always conceded to be by Simone, and certainly its technique seems a serious obstacle to such an attribution. Still, it is a tempting hypothesis that our painter, innovator that he was, might also have introduced such new folklike themes, whose naïve freshness is so unlike the solemn nobility of previous Sienese art. The beds with their bright patterned covers are very much in Simone's taste, and even if he himself was not the painter, the inspiration certainly came from him, so that if the notion of an artist's "circle" ever has any meaning, it unquestionably does in this case.

PIETRO LORENZETTI (d. 1348?) (?) *Scene from the Life of the Blessed Umiltà*, from the altarpiece of the Blessed Umiltà · 1316 (?) · Tempera on panel · $17\frac{1}{2} \times 12\frac{1}{2}''$ · Uffizi Gallery, Florence

This delightful altar painting recounts the life of a woman of medieval times who was beatified. She was Rosanese Negosanti, spouse of Ugolotto Caccianemici, who lived in Faenza and founded there the Order of the Daughters of Vallombrosa, herself assuming the name in religion of "Humility." This painting's authorship has been hotly debated, and even the date inscribed on it has been questioned. It has finally been awarded to Pietro Lorenzetti, of whose activities before 1320 we have no precise knowledge.

PIETRO LORENZETTI *Virgin and Child* · c. 1326–30 · Fresco ·
Lower Church, Basilica of San Francesco, Assisi

The first sure evidence of Pietro Lorenzetti is in a polyptych made
for Arezzo, signed and dated 1320. Its central panel contains a
Madonna of the Hodegitria type, wearing a mantle similar to
those coming into fashion at the court of Burgundy. On the
basis of that picture plus another polyptych, signed and dated
1329 and painted for the monastery of the Carmelites at Siena, a
number of attributions have been made to Lorenzetti, who is,
without doubt, the artist most difficult to pin down of his entire
century. These attributions include the frescoes in the left
transept of the Lower Church in Assisi. More or less contemporary with Simone Martini's frescoes in the same church, they are
radically different in spirit. Their severe expressionism, with no
indulgence in the merely picturesque, gave rise to a current
which, in the next century, was to constitute one of the most
striking and typical aspects of Sienese art in its ultimate phase.

PIETRO LORENZETTI *The Deposition from the Cross* · c. 1326–30 ·
Fresco · Lower Church, Basilica of San Francesco, Assisi

In the same transept, on the end wall and alongside an *En-
tombment*, this *Deposition* belongs to a not very extensive cycle on
the Passion which begins with a large *Crucifixion*. The tragic
expressionism favored by this painter takes on greater breadth
here than elsewhere in his work, and no longer derives only from
a particular treatment of faces and expressions, as in the *Virgin and
Child* (page 131), but also from contortion of the lines of the
bodies and from the exaggerated proportions of those details the
artist wishes to stress. The focus is on the shattered, twisted body
of Christ, but the emotional impact is accentuated by the
grouping of the other figures into a dynamic pyramid shape
within which lines are broken at right angles as well as by the
132 asymmetry of the group in relation to the Cross in the center.

PIETRO LORENZETTI *St. Albert Gives the Carmelite Rule to St. Brocardo* · Central predella panel from the polyptych for the Church of the Carmine · 1329 · Pinacoteca, Siena

Pietro Lorenzetti, who duly signed this polyptych, did not always avoid the picturesque note but, as was the custom, reserved it for the predella, which in this work is placed below a queenly Virgin enthroned, magnificent in style albeit a little stiff and formal. It is exceptional to find in the predella a subject as important as the consignment of the Rule, the most important event in the history of a religious order, but despite the solemnity of the theme, Pietro went so far as to place alongside a splendid and rigorously disposed procession a number of picturesque details, some drawn from observation of everyday reality, some from the creative fancy without which no artist can be considered complete. Here such details introduce a more pleasant note into Lorenzetti's somber tragic universe.

PIETRO LORENZETTI *The Birth of the Virgin* · Two panels from an altarpiece · 1342 · Tempera on panel · Museo dell'Opera del Duomo, Siena

Thirteen years separate this triptych from the altarpiece for the Carmelites, thirteen years during which, to judge by a *Maestà* from as late as 1340, Pietro went on painting his enthroned Virgins who, for all that they are organized according to the conventions of the "noble" style, are surprisingly sensitive and even petulant in expression. What explains the abrupt change of style in this panel, which is signed and is therefore certainly by Pietro? The example of Simone Martini? Of his brother Ambrogio? The wish to be "up-to-date"? Or simply the awakening of tendencies long dormant in him, already hinted at in the Carmine predella, and to which he finally gave free rein at a time when the public was beginning to concede that a genre scene could also be the main subject of a picture?

AMBROGIO LORENZETTI (d. 1348?) *Virgin of the Milk* · c. 1320 ·
Tempera on panel · 35½ × 17¾″ · Seminary of San Francesco,
Siena

Pietro's brother Ambrogio had long been aware of what was
happening. If this charming Virgin nursing a frail Child is
attributed to him, it is precisely because the general tendency of
his temperament was quite opposite to that of his brother and,
in a sense, was rather more like Simone Martini's in its love for
detail and lavish costume. To this he added his own taste for
things observed in everyday life, though he never failed to interpret these in his own imaginative fashion, as here. True, even in
his full maturity he at times had to bow to the taste of a conservative clientele, especially when commissions came from
monasteries.

Ambrogio Lorenzetti *The Submission of St. Louis of Toulouse* ·
c. 1331 · Fresco · San Francesco, Siena

In his youth Ambrogio went to Florence, and that experience
no doubt had some influence on this fresco and its companion
piece, all that remain of the decorations of the cloister of San
Francesco, which were transported to the interior of the church
in 1517 when the cloister was demolished. We know the authorship through Ghiberti, and if he was especially enthusiastic
about this work it was certainly because he recognized in it traits
characteristic of his native Florence. Not that there is servile
imitation of Giotto, but rather an application of theories no
doubt current in Florentine circles, theories which were perhaps
already concerned with cubic space; how to represent it on a
two-dimensional surface, how to dispose various planes in depth.
Much more than with Giotto, one finds here a deliberate use of
these notions. Despite its conscious concern with theory, the
fresco reveals an audacity and breadth of vision which justify its
attribution to the great innovator of Siena.

136

AMBROGIO LORENZETTI *The Effects of Good Government on the City*
(portion) · c. 1338 · Fresco · Palazzo Pubblico, Siena

A few years later Ambrogio turned his back on the too-constricting
example of Florence to reveal the true measure of his own
independent genius. Wishing to proclaim its desire for peace, the
commune of Siena commissioned from him a fresco for the
town hall, an allegory of Good Government and its beneficial
effects on city and countryside. Ambrogio undertook to do what
no Italian painter before him had so much as thought of doing:
to *depict*, rather than to symbolize by conventional means, a city
and a landscape. And yet, there must be no confusion about the
term "depict": what he produced was an intellectual realization
in which real elements were organized not according to what
could be observed but rather on the basis of an intellectual
evocation of something everyone knew. Where a Giotto or a
Simone Martini let city or country be symbolized by some
edifice or a tree so that it was no more than background or stage
setting, Ambrogio totally transformed traditional values to
create a cityscape and a landscape with an existence of their own. 137

AMBROGIO LORENZETTI *The Effect of Good Government on the City*
(continuation) · c. 1338 · Fresco · Palazzo Pubblico, Siena

This is another aspect of Ambrogio's depiction of the city.
The preceding portion showed how the city rises out of the
countryside, how they are linked and interdependent. Here we
have the city itself, inspired no doubt by Siena, with its tall
buildings crammed within battlements in typical medieval fashion.
It is not unlikely that certain buildings were painted "from life,"
and the appearance of tall towers lording over the urban complex,
if not exact in its details, is most probably, at least in over-all
effect, much like what Siena must have looked like observed
from some particular viewpoint. But anyone who tries to take
it as a realistic picture of the old city finds it impossible to pin
down the spot from which it was painted. The city is seen both
138 from above and below: an intellectual viewpoint, not a real one.

AMBROGIO LORENZETTI *The Effects of Good Government on the City*
(continuation) · c. 1338 · Fresco · Palazzo Pubblico, Siena

In a continuously unrolling picture, following the depiction of
the city with its manifold activities, comes a view of the country
around Siena represented in the same arbitrary manner which
organizes real observed elements—hills and brick kilns, fields and
roads—in a concise view, intellectually conceived but recognizable. In evoking with evident pleasure the commercial, rural,
and folk activities of these places, Ambrogio's taste shows itself
quite unlike that of a Simone Martini still caught up in dreams
of chivalry. What he obviously enjoyed painting was the joyous
bustle of a people working hard at building the city's future, and
he left to his pupils the less attractive task of the companion
fresco which shows war as the effect of bad government and
which, had he so desired, could have been the pretext for a
display of military pomp and splendor.

PACINO DI BONAGUIDA (active first quarter of 14th century) *The Tree of the Holy Cross* · Tempera on panel · 99¼ × 60¼″ · Accademia, Florence

We have seen that in Siena there was a diversity of artistic trends due in equal measure to the tastes and temperaments of individual artists and to the demands of the particular public for which they painted. This painting by a contemporary of Giotto proves that an archaic current lingered on alongside the revolutionary efforts. Its interest is chiefly iconographic: inspired by the *Lignum Vitae* of St. Bonaventure, this picture illustrates a doctrine and a legend and was to be the prototype for a long series of productions of the same sort.

TADDEO GADDI (d. c. 1366) *The Nativity* · c. 1332–34 · Tempera
on panel · Medallion from the sacristy chests of Santa Croce ·
Accademia, Florence

This docile pupil of Giotto, considered after his master's death
the best painter in Florence, likewise executed together with his
workshop a *Tree of Life* inspired by St. Bonaventure. But his
crowning work was the frescoes in the Baroncelli Chapel in the
Basilica of Santa Croce and, probably around the same time,
twenty-six quadrilobate medallions and two half-lunettes for the
sacristy cupboards in the same church, today scattered through
various museums. In this idyllic image the artist's chief concern is
with a pleasing arrangement of figurative elements by now well
fixed in the standard repertory of painters of Christian subjects.
It shows how Giotto's art became transformed by his best
disciples. We are told that Sienese influence counted for much in
this, but we might just as well admit that those who follow
obediently in a great man's path end up, inevitably, as not very
creative academics. 141

Master of the Vaults of San Francesco *The Nativity* · Before
1325 · Fresco · Lower Church, Basilica of San Francesco, Assisi

A few years earlier, another painter of Giotto's circle, whose
name has not come down to us, treated the same theme on the
vaults of the Lower Church of San Francesco in Assisi. His
version has the same idyllic character but deserves credit for
being the first. The delicious freshness of its coloring and its
spontaneous and charming naïveté compensate for its dependence
on a master of more forceful personality. In any case, that dependence is less complete than Taddeo Gaddi's, or at least less
servile. While certain elements such as the rock and the manger
and a figure like the St. Joseph derive from Giotto, the artist
also kept in mind the blues and the golden haloes of the miniature
painters and the way they grouped angels into clusters and
arabesques. A personal invention, the little foreground inset of the
Birth of the Virgin, does much toward making this work both
complex and highly attractive.

ANDREA DI CIONE ARCAGNOLO, called ORCAGNA (documented 1343–68) *Christ Conferring Authority on St. Peter and Thomas Aquinas* · 1357 · Tempera on panel · Santa Maria Novella, Florence

Commissioned by the great Strozzi family from the prosperous workshop of the Cione, and signed by the workshop master usually known as Orcagna, this altarpiece takes us out of the Francescan climate so dominant in the Florentine paintings we have been looking at. The times had changed. The Dominicans claimed that the terrible plague which decimated the population of Florence was a punishment from God and that they alone knew the secret of protecting the city from a second onslaught of such a calamity. This gave them the upper hand over the Franciscans who, in addition, were still hampered by the heterodoxy of their minor orders. This altarpiece made for Santa Maria Novella, the Dominican stronghold, is above all a doctrinal proclamation asserting the excellence of the Dominican order: Christ enthroned bestows a book on St. Thomas Aquinas, the second patron of the Order after St. Dominic, and the keys of Paradise on St. Peter, symbol of the Church of Rome, thereby symbolizing the perfect agreement between the two forces. 143

ANDREA DA FIRENZE (documented 1343–77) *The Government of the Church* · c. 1366–67 · Fresco · Spanish Chapel, Santa Maria Novella, Florence

While Pisa was satisfied to commission pictures from those artists of Florence or Milan or Bologna who had taken to wandering about to wherever work was available, the more energetic city of Florence preferred to exert a more active control. For a new chapel, founded by the husband of a plague victim and later used as the chapter house of the Dominican order, a grandiose decoration was ordered to illustrate how the punishment of God could be avoided: under the auspices of the solemn Order, preaching brothers—depicted both in human form and as the dogs of the Lord (*Domini Canes*)—go off in search of the faithful, whom they lead in gracious procession step by step to the very Gates of Paradise guarded by St. Peter and dominated by the Christ of Judgment. The very happy solution by which the artist triumphed over the difficulties in laying out such a complex subject wins him a place among the great painters.

ANDREA DA FIRENZE *The Road to Calvary* (detail) · c. 1366–67
· Fresco · Spanish Chapel, Santa Maria Novella, Florence

The talent of Andrea is confirmed by this fragment from another
fresco in the Spanish Chapel which depicts the Passion of Christ
in the great span of a half-circle. Compared with works of the
preceding generation—those of Pietro Lorenzetti in Assisi or of
Barna in Siena—this work impresses us by the extraordinary
mastery with which it fills the difficult area of the great arch of the
back wall of the chapel. In the center of the composition Calvary
spreads out beneath a vast sky, and on the ground there is a
veritable swarm of figures—a real innovation in Italian art. It
seems almost as if the next step could only be Mantegna's art,
and yet it took almost a century for the lessons of this precursor
to be assimilated. In this detail from the base of the arch it is the
approach of Giovanni da Milano which is applied. Not before
Masolino (see page 183) was anything like this great open composition attempted again, and until then the usual practice was to
crowd together a great many highly animated figures to suggest a
great space.

145

GHERARDO STARNINA (c. 1360/65–1409/13) (?) *Thebaid* ·
Tempera on panel · $29\frac{1}{2} \times 81\frac{7}{8}''$ · Uffizi Gallery, Florence

Along with the message of active devotion they preached in
Florence, the Dominicans in a city like Pisa, by then a Florentine
province 'but with tendencies toward mysticism, gave their
support to an anchoritic and contemplative movement in order
to cut the ground out from under the Benedictines. The latter
had painters who specialized in depicting their saints, Anthony
the Hermit and Jerome, and among them was Gherardo Starnina,
to whom is now attributed this curious picture long believed to
be by Lorenzo Monaco. It has much in common with the fresco
on the same subject in the Camposanto of Pisa, by Francesco
Traini, whom some still consider the author of this picture
despite its very different technique. Like the various cycles on
the Triumph of Death which were inspired by the plague, these
pictures and many writings on the same theme proclaim that
salvation is to be found only in a contemplative life withdrawn
from the world.

GIOVANNI DA MILANO (documented 1350–69) *The Birth of the Virgin* · Fresco · Rinuccini Chapel, Santa Croce, Florence

Some artists, like Orcagna, Andrea da Firenze, and Starnina, placed themselves at the service of the religious orders. Others, such as this Giovanni who came from Milan, accepted commissions from any source and were more concerned with a fresh approach to traditional themes than with religious or political doctrines. In this curious and touching painting, Giovanni entirely renewed the subject of the Birth of the Virgin, which had tended to remain frozen in the form given it by Pietro Lorenzetti. Not only has the old iconographic disposition been supplanted here by another, but the astonishing stylization of the figures (which anticipate those of Piero della Francesca) and the exploitation of arm movements to enliven a neutral space suggest a strong individual artistic personality. Giovanni was finally eclipsed by Piero della Francesca, whose style is more static, and since his personal synthesis of the static and the dynamic was not explored by later artists, he seems to us today somewhat archaic. 147

BARTOLO DI FREDI (c. 1330–c. 1409/10) *The Adoration of the Magi* · c. 1370 · Tempera on panel · 82¾ × 69″ · Pinacoteca, Siena

In the wake of the brilliant upsurge of Sienese art in the first half of the fourteenth century with the Lorenzettis and Simone Martini, there developed a school of painting in that city which, without attaining the creative power of the great innovators, nevertheless kept alive the values of what, by the second generation, had already become a tradition. Among those artists— Barna, Andrea Vanni, Luca di Tommè—the most vital was certainly Bartolo di Fredi, gifted as he was with an incontestable sensitivity as a colorist. Working in a rather lusterless period, he bridged the gap between two high points and guaranteed a quite respectable continuity to local painting.

The Dormition of the Virgin (detail) · Novgorod workshop, 12th–13th centuries · Tempera on panel · Tretyakov Gallery, Moscow

Dating from more than a half century after *The Annunciation of Ustyug* (page 62), this monumental composition, also painted in tempera on wood, tells us much about the still poorly understood characteristics of Russian icons. It will be noted that movement was very soon added to the inward expression of the figures without, however, taking its place as it usually did elsewhere. The great simplicity of means and, above all, of effects, and the emphasis on individualism in the faces, which contrasts with the hieratic rigor of the attitudes, confer on this work a character of greatness. Nevertheless, the icon remains an image summoning men to prayer, a type of figuration entirely unlike that of the Occidental miniature. 149

The Journey to Bethlehem · 14th century · Mosaic · Narthex, Church of the Saviour in Chora (Kariye Camii), Istanbul

Our chronological survey of the monuments of medieval painting helps us to trace the conservative line to which certain of them belong. The decoration of the narthex of the Church of the Saviour in Chora constitutes a great cycle, highly successful as a whole. The finesse and virtuosity of the Byzantine mosaic artists remained remarkable, but a century after their high point it becomes obvious that their conception of an image derived from the miniaturists, and that thenceforth the avant-garde was to be found elsewhere, in the Italian workshops and those of the French court. However perfect the rendering, it cannot conceal the immobility of the conception or the traditionalism of the figurative elements used.

Christ in Limbo · 14th century · Mosaic · Church of the Saviour in Chora (Kariye Camii), Istanbul

The decoration of the edifice includes two great cycles, one the story of Jesus and Mary, the other the miracles of Christ. There are unmistakably two manners, two workshops, and although they worked with different means they were both less concerned with theological matters than with clear exposition of the narrative. Thus, the fact that notions from the Apocrypha are introduced is less striking than the contrast in the two manners, one related to the dominant style in the Western Mediterranean, the other to Greek and Slavic art. Further, in one of the series a painterly approach is exploited, rather than the techniques more appropriate to mosaic.

The Nativity · 14th century · Fresco · Church of Peripleptos, Mistra

The frescoes in Mistra were executed in the fourteenth century for the despots of Morea. To understand them, one must keep in mind their setting: they loom up out of darkness on the vaults of tiny churches and were designed to be viewed from below at the proper angle. What is interesting here is the transition in the Eastern Mediterranean from the Greek school—the *maniera greca*—to the icon. This same composition is found in many Russian works, and apparently such models were disseminated widely by itinerant workshops, as was also the case in the West.

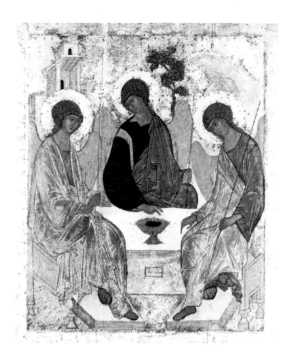

ANDREI RUBLEV *The Trinity* · 1422–27 · Tempera on panel ·
$55\frac{1}{2} \times 44\frac{1}{2}''$ · From the Monastery of the Trinity-and-St.-Sergius
at Zagorsk, near Moscow · Tretyakov Gallery, Moscow

Contemporary of Masolino, the Limbourg brothers, and the
Master of Flémalle, Andrei Rublev represents the great Eastern
tradition in the waning Middle Ages. Two centuries after *The
Dormition of the Virgin* (page 149), Russian art returned to a vision
stripped of all striving for effect. The same subject was treated in
Paris in the thirteenth century (page 95) in an entirely different
spirit. The work of Rublev is not inspired by a written text but
by a living thought. Monumentality is achieved by an organization of space and an equilibrium between planes of color which
were to remain unknown in the West until modern times.

The Annunciation · Icon from the Church of St. Clement, Ohrid · 16th century · Tempera on panel · Museum, Skopje, Yugoslavia

Comparison of this *Annunciation* with that of Ustyug (page 62) shows how widely apart in feeling they are and also how an art can evolve within a system which is both unified and diversified and still remain faithful to a set style. In place of a simple face-to-face confrontation of the two personages, here they are infused with animation and surrounded by a wealth of accessories. The architectural element defines the setting as a church. References and associations spring from the narrative and action and not, as in the past, from meditation on an article of faith. The central concern is no longer the communication of a thought but the perpetuation of an iconographic tradition.

Martyrdom of St. George · c. 1300 · Fresco · Chapel of the Rosary (formerly of St. George), Cathedral, Clermont-Ferrand

St. George is shown at the moment of his ascension rather than of his martyrdom. This is the first appearance of the demigod type of figure later typical of Donatello, and the first conception modeled after the antique. Certainly it lacks perspective, but it does resolve the problem of mental vision in movement and, unlike the Parisian miniature style, challenges us to reconsider the question of the "Gothic" sources of the Renaissance.

The Burial of St. John the Baptist · 1354–62 · Fresco · Chartreuse, Villeneuve-lès-Avignon

The Chapel of St. John the Baptist was the initial edifice around which the great Carthusian monastery was built. Its frescoes form a complete cycle recently attributed to the Italian Matteo Giovanetti. In any event, they have some connection with the foliage-design tapestries of northern France, and the recent discovery of the frescoes of Simone Martini, who died in 1344, proves the existence of a Franco-Italian center of great influence. Was not the culture of Petrarch and Giotto born of contacts between France and Italy?

GIRARD D'ORLÉANS *Portrait of John II the Good* · c. 1360–64 ·
Tempera on panel · 23¼ × 14¼″ · The Louvre, Paris

To this artist is also attributed the famous painted altarcloth
from Narbonne which includes portraits of Charles V and his
Queen. The two works indicate the King's interest in art as
ornament for the royal chapels and palaces. Here we have one
of the first portraits as such in the history of post-classical art.
The subject is portrayed with astonishing presence, and the
work certainly owes something to the statues and tomb sculpture
of the time. Besides, it is one of the very first easel paintings
known. It opens the way to one of the realistic phases of Western
art not so much for its style as such as in its aims.

The Adoration of the Magi · Parisian workshop, c. 1380 (?) ·
Tempera on panel · 19½ × 12″ · National Museum, Florence

This wing from a small diptych known as the *Bargello Altarpiece*
is halfway between the Parisian miniatures of the thirteenth
century and Gentile da Fabriano, and is a perfect illustration of
the international style of the end of the fourteenth century.
Scholars one after the other have spoken of relationships with
Siena, Bohemia, Flanders, or Avignon, and this in itself testifies
to a common style throughout Europe dominated by the taste
and intellectual culture of Paris.

Christ Bearing the Cross · School of Avignon, c. 1390 · Tempera
on panel · 15 × 11″ · The Louvre, Paris

Comparison of this work with the preceding clarifies what was
said there. The over-all tonality and a greater breadth in drawing
recall the style of the *Burial of St. John* from Avignon and of
Simone Martini. The influence of the international style was
widespread: in England, for example, it appears in the Wilton
Diptych. Rather than insisting on Parisian workshops, one
should speak of the princely style of the French court, not only
the model of the time but the rallying point for artists as much as
for great lords.

MELCHIOR BROEDERLAM *The Annunciation* and *The Visitation* ·
Left wing of the Champmol Altarpiece · 1394–99 · Tempera on
panel · 64 × 51″ · Museum of Fine Arts, Dijon

This altarpiece was painted for the Burgundians. Despite the
similarity of figurative material, it is certain that here we are in
another artistic climate than that of Paris. The composition is less
all of one piece; the coloring is richer; architectural motifs play
a more important role, especially because they exploit space in
depth and thereby anticipate the great scientific codification of
160 the Italian Quattrocento.

MELCHIOR BROEDERLAM *The Circumcision* and *The Flight into Egypt* · Right wing of the Champmol Altarpiece · 1394–99 · Tempera on panel · 64 × 51″ · Museum of Fine Arts, Dijon

It is interesting to pick out in this and the following pictures the common elements: the Fountain of Life as in the Limbourgs, the architecture of the Master of Flémalle, the rock formations of the Italians. Between the Parisian, Sienese, and Florentine style of 1360–80 and the Renaissance of Masaccio and Van Eyck, there came a generation which throughout Europe exchanged themes and suggestions.

JEAN MALOUEL *The Small Pietà* · c. 1400 · Tempera on panel ·
The Louvre, Paris

Between Broederlam and Bellechose, the official painter of the
Dukes of Burgundy at Dijon, was Malouel. The two *Pietàs*
attributed to him, the Small and the Great, show how much
Burgundian art was indebted to that of Paris. For some years now
it has been suggested that the *Madonna* in the Berlin Museum
may also be by him. That picture is itself most exceptional and
as much a unique innovation as the portrait of John the Good,
since it is painted with tempera on canvas instead of board.
Most probably it was in the circle of the dukes of the royal house
of France that portable paintings destined not for altars, but
intended merely as separate devotional images, became common,
and this was owing to the itinerant living habits which also led the
162 nobility to sponsor tapestry workshops.

HENRI BELLECHOSE *Altarpiece of the Martyrdom of St. Denis* ·
1416 · Tempera on panel · $63\frac{1}{4} \times 82\frac{1}{2}''$ · The Louvre, Paris

Bellechose had just succeeded Malouel as painter to Jean Sans
Peur when he was charged with completing this unfinished
altarpiece. With it a new generation appears. Compared with the
Christ Bearing the Cross of Avignon (page 159), this work is still
very Parisian, and its character is traditional in contrast to
Broederlam's style. Parisian style of this period must be sought
elsewhere, in miniatures and tapestries.

Hennequin of Bruges and Nicolas Bataille *The Whore of Babylon*, from the Apocalypse Tapestries · 1373–79 · Château, Angers

Duke Louis I of Anjou borrowed from the royal library of Charles V a manuscript of the Apocalypse as model for this marvelous set of tapestries in which are summed up the learning and taste of the last Gothic generations. They were finally bestowed on the Cathedral of Angers bij King René, as the most precious testimony to the prestige of his house. In them a veritable world of dreams unfolds before us. It must be kept in mind that in those times men occupied austere dwellings that were enlivened by tapestries with foliage designs which they even transported with them on their travels. In this set, tapestries with blue and rose backgrounds alternate, and there are both realism and mystery in them. Tapestry, miniatures, and stained glass were 164 the basis for one of the greatest periods in the history of painting.

The Lady and the Unicorn · End of 15th century · Tapestry · Musée de Cluny, Paris

Although this work is very much later in date than the others in this chapter, it has been included as a concrete reminder that the Middle Ages did not die out suddenly at the start of the fifteenth century, either in men's tastes or in their ways of thinking. Executed for the Le Vistes and the Guillards, great lawyers of the region of Lyons, these splendid tapestries combine the theme of the symbolic figuration of the five senses with the by then legendary subject of the magic hunt. The Middle Ages faded away into legend, but for a long time the visual stuff for works of the imagination continued to be medieval. 165

Between 1380 and 1422, under Charles VI, Paris, or more correctly the French court, was more than ever the most refined art center of Europe. Duc Jean de Berry in particular was a great patron of artists, and it was through him that, in rivalry with the Burgundians, the French workshops continued their creative activity. André Beauneveu, Jacquemart de Hesdin, Jacques Coene, Jean Malouel, the Limbourg brothers, and the anonymous Masters of the Hours of Boucicaut and of Rohan are in no way inferior to an Orcagna, an Andrea da Firenze, a Giovanni de' Grassi.

Master of the Hours of Boucicaut *The Visitation*, from the
Book of Hours of the Maréchal de Boucicaut · c. 1410–15 ·
Miniature · Musée Jacquemart-André, Paris

Among the painters of the Duc de Berry, this master is one of
the least recognized although his works are of immense interest.
It is obvious here that, long before Masolino and Masaccio,
knowledge of linear perspective was spreading throughout
Europe. There is no need to stress the virtuosity of the way it is
associated here with other ways of representing space, or how the
iridescent sky and chiaroscuro anticipate all of the solutions of the
entire Quattrocento.

Master of the Hours of Boucicaut *Presentation Ceremony*, from
the book by Pierre Salmon, *Lamentations sur son état* · 1409 ·
Miniature · Musée de Cluny, Paris

This scene of the presentation of the book to its patron owes
something to the theater for its conception; and it contrasts
markedly with the preceding examples because of its simultaneous exposition of scenes occurring at different times. Evidently
in this milieu no attempt was made to impose a single method.
This was an art directed to readers of lively intelligence, and
figurative means became limited only when times changed and
there came about a change in the aims of art and in its public.

THE LIMBOURG BROTHERS *The Month of June: Paris and the Palace*, from *Les Très Riches Heures du Duc de Berry* · 1413–16 · Miniature · Musée Condé, Chantilly

The Limbourg brothers were in the service of the Duke of Burgundy from 1402 to 1404, then for a time in the Paris workshops, and after 1410 employed by the Duc de Berry. To them we owe certain masterpieces of miniature art which were also of capital importance in the development of the international style of the beginning of the fifteenth century. Jean de Berry was one of the most lavish art patrons in history. It was at his court that the convergence of all contemporary styles—Italian, Flemish, Burgundian—was best realized, and it was there that the solutions were found which were to result in the great Franco-Flemish and Italian works of the early Quattrocento. 169

THE LIMBOURG BROTHERS *The Month of July: Poitiers and the Palace*, from *Les Très Riches Heures du Duc de Berry* · 1413–16 · Miniature · Musée Condé, Chantilly

This book of hours presents a synthesis of the medieval system of intellectual representation with modern pictorial techniques. On the one hand, the astrological calendar expresses the relationship of man to the universe of which he is one element indissolubly attached to the whole. On the other, the direct interest in the depiction of men's activities, the importance placed on the organic connection of the picture with the entire page, the evocation of the transparency of air, all these belong to a system of values destined to sustain the modern age.

Master of the Hours of Rohan *The Dead Man before His Judge*, from *Les Heures de Rohan* · c. 1420 · Miniature · Ms. lat. 9471, Bibliothèque Nationale, Paris

Alongside the skillful compositions of the Master of the Hours of Boucicaut and the picturesque scenes of the Limbourg brothers we cannot omit this striking expressionistic page, archaic perhaps in its over-all design and lack of spatial depth, but at the same time a presage, both in sentiment and in the extraordinary realism of the dying man, of the most modern manifestations of Western art in the succeeding centuries.

STEFANO DA VERONA (1374–after 1438) *Madonna of the Rose Garden* · c. 1395–1400 (?) · Tempera on panel · 50¾ × 37½″ · Castelvecchio, Verona

This version of the Madonna of Humility, seated on the ground in a closed and intimate garden, seems most unusual in Italian art, whose usual repertory of decorative motifs includes neither the flowered greensward, the little garden, the bird-winged angels, nor the birds themselves. True, the Master of Vico l'Abate had attempted to draw attention to incidental notes borrowed from nature and not indispensable to the story depicted, but his approach was quite different: his details are magnified, isolated, and expressive, whereas here they are abundant, finely worked out, and entwined in arabesques recalling the goldsmith's craft or a certain type of tapestry.

Stefano da Verona *The Adoration of the Magi* · 1435 · Tempera
on panel · The Brera, Milan

This work, the only one Stefano signed and dated, serves along
with two frescoes signed but not dated as the basis for all other
attributions to him. This painting reveals the impact of diverse
influences and how they were harmonized. In it we see how the
aging Stefano came under the sway of the Umbrian painter
Gentile da Fabriano, dead by then but famed throughout Italy
for his *Adoration of the Magi* of 1423. Obvious as the borrowings
from Gentile are (compare the plate on page 175), it seems that
for the scene of homage the artist turned back to the painting on
the same subject by Bartolo di Fredi of Siena (page 148).   173

GENTILE DA FABRIANO (c. 1370–1427) *St. Dominic* · Detail from the polyptych of Valle Romita · c. 1400 · Tempera on panel · The Brera, Milan

In his first works Gentile was not yet equipped with the vast culture which later was to permit him to deal with the procedures and sentiments of the past as if they were his own and to assimilate and give visual form to the most recent viewpoints on art and history. This polyptych shows that around 1400 Gentile was still no more than a limited provincial painter. Nevertheless, he was able to endow his personages with an esoteric spirituality while at the same time playing with consummate mastery with oppositions of broad simple volumes and carefully studied naturalistic details.

GENTILE DA FABRIANO *The Adoration of the Magi* · 1423 · Tempera on panel · 9′ 10⅛″ × 9′ 3″ · Uffizi Gallery, Florence

Gentile had numerous bonds with both Venice and Verona, as well as with Florence, Siena, and Lombardy. This altarpiece, his masterwork, is at one and the same time a synthesis of all his hesitations before diverse ways and also a masterful demonstration that a great artist can overcome all such confusions, even if he never finds the single solution to sweep them all away. Gentile wished to sacrifice nothing of the treasures accumulated in his peripatetic life: neither the splendor of Venice, last vestige of the Byzantinism it loved; nor Sienese density and expressionism as seen in the procession here; nor the humanism of Florence as reflected in the foreground figures; nor Veronese naturalism, which he raised to a high point here in the dogs, horses, camels, the ass, and the ox; nor finally the latest innovation, the rationalistic perspective he applied within the lunettes of the gold frame and in the predella. Such a mixture might easily have resulted in disaster. It did not, and this masterpiece comes to us as the product of a great talent and a vast personal culture.

GENTILE DA FABRIANO *The Presentation in the Temple*, from the
predella of the preceding altarpiece · 1423 · Tempera on panel ·
$10\frac{1}{4} \times 24''$ · The Louvre, Paris

The predella of the *Adoration* was dismembered, and one of its
panels is now in the Louvre. In Gentile's time, as in the past, the
predella continued to be the chosen site for avant-garde experi-
ment: audacious essays, innovations too daring for the main
body of an altarpiece—which had to be in a noble style consecrated by tradition—these were relegated to the predella. When
the noble style was still Byzantine-influenced and hieratic, the
predella was used for flights of fancy, but in Gentile's time it
was the Gothic with all its romanticism and fantasy which was
deemed noble, and so the independence and progressivism
typical of the predella took the form of "scientific" rigor. These
carefully organized architectural elements with something of
the antique about them, these elongated, stylized, and impassive
figures which in a few years would be promoted to the place of
honor—the central panels of altarpieces—all prove that in
forward-looking circles there was already concern with perspective and the revival of the antique, though it was not until
around the middle of the century that they finally came to be
176 considered essential.

GENTILE DA FABRIANO *The Young King* · Detail from *The Adoration of the Magi* · 1423 · Tempera on panel · Uffizi Gallery, Florence

Between Gentile's *St. Dominic* and this *Young King* intervened the influence of Venice. Gentile lived also in Brescia, where he was caught up in the Lombard craze for the French romances of chivalry and the fashions of the court of Burgundy. Finally, he must certainly have been familiar with Sienese art. All these diverse experiences are concentrated in the figure of the young king. Here the theatrical vision of knights-of-old was not conjured up as a real knight, but rather to lend glory to the young son of the powerful Strozzi family, which held the reins of industry in Florence and which commissioned this altarpiece. 177

MASTER OF ASCIANO *The Birth of the Virgin* · c. 1430–40 ·
Tempera on panel · $87\frac{3}{8} \times 62\frac{1}{4}''$ · Museum, Asciano

To emphasize the international character of the system of
representation in favor throughout Europe in the first third of
the fifteenth century, we have placed side by side here works
from Italy and Flanders. This anonymous painting from Asciano
carries on the creative effort of the Sienese, who are incorrectly
judged archaic because they perpetuated certain medieval values.
This work takes up again the theme of a painting by Pietro
Lorenzetti, and of a fresco he and his brother did for the hospital
of the Scale in Siena. There are air and space in this picture and
perspective, a figure draped in gold brocade in the fashion of
Burgundy, a bird-winged angel gleaming in the entrance; these
new elements serve to re-create that climate of intimacy and
domestic peace which, though with other means, was another
aspect of the Sienese genius. Further, the warm-cool quality of
the coloring makes of it a work unique in its time.

MASTER OF FLÉMALLE *The Marriage of the Virgin* · c. 1425 ·
Tempera on panel · $30\frac{3}{4} \times 35\frac{1}{2}''$ · The Prado, Madrid

At almost the same time but at the other end of Europe, another
anonymous master painted this picture, which is in many ways
both like and unlike the preceding. It belongs to a group of
works which are highly problematical: are they by Robert
Campin, Rogier van der Weyden in his youth, someone else, or
several artists? The one sure fact is that, alongside the Van
Eycks and before 1430, when we find Rogier in full possession
of his gifts, there was a Northern style which carried out the
same experiments as the Italians in pushing still further the
ultimate discoveries of the international workshops of the
waning Middle Ages. A key work, the so-called *Mérode Altarpiece*,
is much closer than the *Nativity* of the Master of Flémalle to the
painting in Asciano in terms of structure, although it is also more
related to the Van Eycks and, despite its incomparable quality,
less revealing of the difficulties the innovators had to overcome. 179

MASTER OF FLÉMALLE *The Nativity* · c. 1430 · Tempera on panel ·
$34\frac{1}{4} \times 27\frac{5}{8}''$ · Museum of Fine Arts, Dijon

Comparison of this and the preceding painting shows the
hesitations experienced in this milieu. In *The Marriage of the
Virgin* two episodes are juxtaposed and, in line with medieval
tradition, the events of the narrative are set forth in separate
scenes, as are also the two aspects of vision which bring together
the interior and exterior of an edifice whose portal is that of the
Church of the Sablon in Brussels and whose choir is an imaginary
Jerusalem. The unity of the picture depends therefore on intellectual associations. In the present painting, however, optical
integration is pushed further. The approach remains intellectual,
but it has sloughed off the tradition of simultaneous events. The
unity of the world of the senses was soon to supplant the unity
of the world of thought.

MASOLINO DA PANICALE (1383–1440/47) *The Foundation of Santa Maria Maggiore* · c. 1430 · Tempera on panel · $56\frac{3}{4} \times 29\frac{7}{8}''$ · National Gallery of Capodimonte, Naples

The celestial vision is set in a qualitative, unmeasured, typically medieval space, while the earthly vision is one of the first Italian examples of linear perspective governed by a single vanishing point. It cannot be supposed that the invention of linear perspective and modern notions of space were achieved suddenly in 1425 by the Florentines. Renaissance art was the product of an international culture which grew out of the last experiments of the Gothic; moreover, it did not restrict itself to a single approach.

Masolino *Herod's Banquet* · 1435 · Fresco · Baptistery, Castiglione Olona

Even a few years later, in the period following Masaccio's death when he was full master of his own art, Masolino continued to combine very modern and very traditional elements of representation. The open loggia in the foreground goes back to the setting for the Tabitha episode in the Brancacci Chapel frescoes, while the colonnade resembles the earliest architectural exploits of Michelozzo in Venice and in the monastery of San Marco in Florence. These elements clash with a background which is not governed by the same principle and is less integrated than in Flemish paintings. What orders the imagination of artists is not merely an ability to look at the universe and then transfer what is seen to a two-dimensional surface by means of tricks of illusion. Rather, and much more important, it is a matter of how they conceive the association of elements containing inherent significance and how they articulate them within a whole.

MASOLINO *The Crucifixion* · 1428–31 · Fresco · San Clemente,
Rome

Dated between 1428 and 1431, and therefore earlier than the
Banquet, this admirable work is infinitely more modern and more
integrated in the direction to be taken by the so-called Grand
Style of the future. Yet it was executed for the same patron,
Cardinal Castiglione, and moreover recalls the approach of
Andrea da Firenze in the 1360s in a similar monumental fresco
(page 145). To produce true art, artists need more than a handy
system. Not before Mantegna's *Crucifixion*, from about 1460, did
the principle of open space in a landscape which dips and rises
again become one of the standard solutions of modern art. For
at least two generations, painters explored a diversity of approaches
before arriving finally at systems which, soon after, turned into
academic formulas. 183

LORENZO VENEZIANO (documented 1356–72) *The Annunciation* ·
Central panel of a polyptych · 1359 · Tempera on panel · 49⅝ ×
29½″ · Accademia, Venice

It was only in the generation following Paolo Veneziano that the
local Byzantinism began to become less clear-cut. A style developed which was more fluid but also heavier and rather flaccid.
As yet Venice took no more from International Gothic than its
way of treating draperies and a certain suppleness in posing
figures, but not its sparkling vivacity. This Virgin of the Annunciation is no longer the humble handmaid of God as in
Byzantium and Siena but instead is a queen as in Western art, and
the angel here is a submissive messenger who bows before the
184 future Mother of Christ.

Cenni di Francesco di Ser Cenni *The Stigmatization of St.
Francis* · 1410 · Fresco · San Francesco, Volterra

Agnolo Gaddi, Taddeo's son, set up in Florence a large workshop which churned out pictures one after the other for anyone
who would buy. Cenni di Francesco followed his lead, but,
working alone, without assistants, his paintings were much more
personal. In this fresco, where the figure of the Saint is borrowed
from Giotto, he gave free rein to his gift for observation to
construct this delightful vertical background in which a city and
a desert are tumbled together like children's playthings. 185

St. Michael · Detail from a *Last Judgment* · Auvergnat workshop, 1405 · Tempera on panel · Collegiate Church, Ennezat (Puy-de-Dôme)

We have chosen to place this picture between those examples which illustrate the Florentine tradition and the first manifestations of a genuinely Venetian style, and those others which show how Siena made one last effort to revitalize the medieval heritage rather than reject it. In opposition to the styles of the French court, it reveals that in France as in Italy provincial workshops continued to cling to a truly academic medievalism. This vast composition inspired by the Apocalypse offers something like an ultimate summing up of the old traditional figurative themes, though these had more often been treated in sculpture over portals of cathedrals than in paint.

Sassetta (Stefano di Giovanni di Consolo) (1392?–1450)
The Journey of the Magi · c. 1430 · Tempera on panel · 9 × 12″ ·
Metropolitan Museum of Art, New York

The resurgence of Sienese painting took place before and after
the middle of the fifteenth century. Among the greatly gifted
painters responsible for it—Giovanni di Paolo, Sano di Pietro,
the anonymous Masters of the Osservanza, of Asciano, and of the
Life of St. Anthony—the most famous, Sassetta, was also the
one who studied most attentively and conscientiously the
Florentine innovations in linear perspective. Although he did not
adhere to them, they were not entirely banned from his work. In
this picture, Sassetta's attitude toward the Florentine experiments
is revealed by his attempt to create an impression of spatial depth.
However, the effect is not attained by the means favored in
Florence, that is, perspective lines meeting at a fixed point in
infinity plus a horizon line carefully established and set low.
Instead, Sassetta uses empirical means with an invisible but high
horizon line, and much of the charm of the picture is due to this
approach.

SASSETTA *St. Anthony in the Wilderness* · Before 1450 · Tempera on panel · 17¾ × 13⅜″ · Collection Robert Lehman, New York

The same high horizon line characterizes this masterpiece of Sienese Quattrocento painting. It strives to synthesize the notion of distance with the precepts of the Trecento to which the artist, for all his individuality, obviously remained very much attached. The artist discovered the possibilities of curved space (all the lines determining space are curved: the horizon, the clouds, the road leading to the church). He thereby showed that there were other means of rendering space than linear perspective, and that medieval optics were quite capable of working out a system of vision in depth and of three-dimensional space.

Master of Trebon *The Resurrection* · c. 1380 · Tempera on panel · 52 × 36″ · National Gallery, Prague

It must be kept in mind that in the fourteenth and fifteenth centuries Gothic civilization touched every corner of Europe. There was a common Occidental culture at the very moment when new forces were about to write finis to universal beliefs and social and economic conditions built up slowly during the preceding centuries. Bohemia in particular enjoyed a brilliant Gothic culture. This painting was chosen because it shows brilliantly how national geniuses found their individual expression within one of the most consistent systems of thought the world has known.

PISANELLO (ANTONIO DI PUCCI) (before 1395–1455) *The Vision of St. Eustace* · Before 1450 · Tempera on panel · $21\frac{1}{2} \times 25\frac{3}{4}''$ · National Gallery, London

While resistance to Florentine rationalism was strongest and most systematic in Siena, because of its attachment to a past more glorious than that of other regions, it was also present in such places as Verona, which, although not indifferent to new ideas, sought them out from the most remote sources. Pisanello was perfectly capable of exploiting the Florentine experiments when he wished, but his natural bent was to the romantic and, at times, even mystic art of chivalry faded into legend, and to this he joined a courtly style which he himself brought to its highest development. This painting, unanimously attributed to him, disdains all spatial and scientific considerations. It is set in a mystical environment not otherwise defined and yet well characterized, and is, above all, a pretext for studies of animals and the knight's costume, favorite concerns of this artist whose numerous sketches of animals and costumes are among his chief claims to

glory.

PISANELLO *Portrait of Ginevra d'Este* (?) · 1438–40 · Tempera on panel · 17 × 11¾″ · The Louvre, Paris

This marvelous portrait reveals the favorite preoccupations of Pisanello. The profile in silhouette as if cut out by a knife blade, as in the medals of which he also was a great master; the slight displacement from an axis, with the head in full and the body in three-quarter profile; the costume and headdress painstakingly studied and admirably rendered; the background of flowering shrubs; the butterflies—all of these are conceived as pictorial elements and are fitted together entirely as functions of their internal relationships and with no concern for anecdote or situation. The picture is built up on the basis of its own logic, which is that of a proper relationship between forms and colors.

Master of the Pietà of Avignon *Pietà* · c. 1460 · Tempera
on panel · 63¾ × 85⅞" · The Louvre, Paris

While the Italians, by a series of compromises, were striving to
renew the Gothic style which was still vital but already con-
demned by the rise of a point of view less sensitive to inspiration
than to reason, the last Gothic workshops in France were
marking the end of the system which had been dominant in
Europe for three hundred years. With absolute mastery of the
rhythm of line and relief, supreme decorativeness of forms, and
consummate simplicity in rendering a variety of expressions, the
plastic thought of the Gothic produced this final masterwork
before disappearing. The fact remains that this painting is still
closely related to sculpture. If the Gothic had to bow out
before a new style, perhaps it was because, having inspired
admirable works in all media, it remained too dependent on its
specific techniques. In contrast, the new art, often of lesser
quality, emphasized the intellectual bases of a system of thought
that took pride in manipulating the stuff of nature rather than in
working out a style impregnated with the mirages of a universe
conceived in accord with man's own modes of feeling.

INDEX

ACKNOWLEDGMENTS

The following photographers, photographic agencies, and publishers have co-operated in the making and gathering of the color photographs for this book:

Hirmer Verlag, Munich; Editions Pierre Tisné, Paris; La Photothèque, Paris; Photographie Giraudon, Paris; Scala Istituto Fotografico Editoriale, Florence.

The publisher and the author express their gratitude and appreciation to all the museums, libraries, and cultural authorities who so graciously made available for this book the works in their custody or possession. All such sources are acknowledged in the captions for the individual reproductions.